TREKKING

Outside

ADVENTURE TRAVEL

Outside

ADVENTURE TRAVEL

TREKKING

DAVID NOLAND

Outside
BOOKS

W. W. Norton & Company
NEW YORK • LONDON

For information about permission to reproduce selections from this book, write to
Permissions, W. W. Norton & Company, Inc.
500 Fifth Avenue, New York, NY 10110

The text of this book is composed in Perpetua
with the display set in Monkey
Project Management by Julie Stillman
Composition by Sylvie Vidrine
Manufacturing by Dai Nippon Printing Company
Map Illustrations by Janet Fredericks

Book design by Bill Harvey

Library of Congress Cataloging-in-Publication Data

Noland, David.
    Trekking / David Noland.
            p. cm. -- (Outside adventure travel)
    "Outside Books."
    Includes bibliographical references (p.) and index.
    1. Hiking. 2. Mountaineering. I. Title. II. Series.

GV199.5 .N65 2001
796.51--dc21
                                                    00-048117

ISBN 0-393-32072-3 (pbk.)

W. W. Norton & Company, Inc., 500 Fifth Avenue, New York, N.Y. 10110
www.wwnorton.com
W. W. Norton & Company Ltd., 10 Coptic Street, London WC1A 1PU

1 2 3 4 5 6 7 8 9 0

To Callie,
I can hardly wait till you're old enough
to share the joys and challenges of the trail with me.

ACKNOWLEDGMENTS

In the long trek that was the writing of this book, many people shared the load. Virtually every outfitter listed provided information and insights, but particular thanks are due Jim Sano of Geographic Expeditions, who opened his company's financial ledgers for a look at the economics of a typical trek. Leo LeBon of Mountain Travel-Sobek helped me trace the history of trekking. Janet Baldwin, the librarian at the Explorers Club in New York, put that marvelous resource at my disposal. John Barstow, my editor at Norton, adeptly prodded, cajoled, and soothed me through the writing process. I'm grateful for his expertise and enthusiasm.

Special thanks to Vintage Books for allowing me to draw on material from my earlier book, *Travels Along the Edge: 40 Ultimate Adventures for the Modern Nomad.* Thanks also to Pete Warner of the bookstore AdventurousTraveler.com, who let me paw freely through dozens of its volumes during my research.

CONTENTS

Sunset over Machu Picchu, Peru.

INTRODUCTION

Twelve years later, the exhilaration of that moment still resonates. After three days of airplanes, buses, Nairobi hotels, and jeeps juddering along dirt roads, I was desperate to escape man-made artifices, to get out and walk, to immerse myself in the world rather than watch it go by out the window. We arrived at the end of the road, a place called Chogoria, on the lower flanks of Mount Kenya. Porters were already hoisting their loads of food and camping gear.

Eight fellow trekkers and I laced up our boots, shouldered featherlight day packs, and strolled off on a smooth trail into the African wilderness. I breathed in great draughts of cool mountain air as leg muscles unwound. The sun warmed my face through a sharp blue sky. Dinner and a comfortable tent awaited on the shore of a lake a few miles up the trail. Those first steps of my first trek, and the anticipation of what lay ahead, fired my soul as never before.

Forgive the hyberbole, but to me, trekking is a very good approximation of heaven on earth. I love the sense of going somewhere, of a journey to a destination rather than a mere aimless wander. I love the remote landscapes and the local people going about their regular business. I love the walking, the mindless putting of one foot in front of the other for hour after hour. I love the utter distance from my regular life. And, let me be quite frank about this: I love not having to carry a heavy pack, cook, or scrub pots.

Apparently quite a few people share my feelings. Some 75,000 people went trekking last year in Nepal alone. The adventure travel industry, built on the bedrock of trekking, is growing as never before. "Our business was up 50 percent in 1999," says Jim Sano of Geographic Expeditions, a leading trek operator. "And 1999 was up 50 percent over 1998." At the start of the 21st century, the idea of a long unladen journey by foot through remote country is clearly an idea whose time has come.

The word trek comes from South Africa, an old Boer word that meant a journey by ox wagon. In broad usage, it has come to mean any long or arduous journey. It later was used to describe the first commercial hiking trips, supported by Sherpa porters and staff, through the mountains of Nepal. For the purposes of this book, however, we will define trekking this way: *A trek is a long-distance multi-day walk from Point A to Point B (or back to A) during which the walker is required neither to carry heavy loads nor prepare meals.* Although commercial treks have traditionally featured full-service camping and human porters and/or pack animals, our

Opposite: Near Rabang, West Sikkim, India. Above: Hindu ascetic meditates on temple steps, Durbar Square, Kathmandu, Nepal.

definition is broad enough to accept a hut or a trekkers' lodge in place of a tent, a lodge meal in place of a campfire, or a Toyota minivan in place of a yak.

A History of Trekking

Recreational trekking is a fairly recent phenomenon, not even as old as the Beatles. The world's first commercial trek commenced on February 25, 1965, when three Midwestern women of a certain age set off on foot from Panchkai, Nepal bound for Tengboche Monastery, near Mount Everest. Dr. Margaret Prouty, 56, a pediatrician from Madison, Wisconsin; Ruby Dere, 62, a retired bacteriologist, also from Madison; and Frances Mullen, 64, the assistant superintendent of schools in Chicago, walked for 35 days and 150 miles, accompanied by three Sherpa guides, nine porters, and Col. J.O.M. "Jimmy" Roberts, a retired British Indian Army officer.

The women had seen a small ad placed by Roberts (who lived in Pokhara, Nepal) in a 1964 issue of *Holiday* magazine. A veteran mountain climber as well as a career military man, Roberts had opted for service in India and Southeast Asia mainly so he could climb and hike in the Himalayas during his leave time. During World War II, Roberts commanded a company of Gurkhas, the fierce Nepali mercenary soldiers who fought for Britain in Burma and Malaya. Later he became the military attaché at the British Embassy in Kathmandu. While there, Roberts managed to wrangle permission from the King of Nepal to make excursions on foot into areas that were previously off-limits to foreigners. Roberts and

famed British explorer H. W. Tilman walked into the Annapurna region in 1950, and Roberts was later the first Westerner to enter the fabled Annapurna Sanctuary. In 1953, he served as a supply officer on the epochal expedition that sent Hillary and Tenzing to the summit of Everest. During his travels in the mountains of Nepal, Roberts grew to greatly admire the Sherpas, the friendly, hardworking natives of the Everest region who served as porters, guides, and staff on his various excursions.

Upon his retirement from the British Embassy, Roberts stayed on in Nepal. Looking for a way to give his beloved Sherpas (and himself) some regular employment, Roberts hit upon the idea of outfitting walking expeditions into the mountains of Nepal in the traditional style of the British raj. Roberts' inspiration was the sheep-hunting parties in Kashmir that he and fellow British officers had organized for themselves. Local porters or pack animals would carry all the loads and a staff would set up comfortable camps each night. Roberts figured people might pay to see the highest mountain in the world in this relatively comfortable manner, and placed the small ad in *Holiday* for a trek to Everest. The asking price for Roberts' proposed 35-day trek was $450.

The three women loved their trek to Everest. "I remember Margaret raving about the scenery and the wonderful people she met," recalls Shirley Cuccia, who worked with Dr. Prouty at the time. "I still have a teacup she brought me." (It should be pointed out that Prouty and her friends were not your typical grandmothers. Two were experienced mountain

Photo opportunity on Mount Kilimanjaro, Tanzania, East Africa.

climbers, and Roberts wrote many years later that "a more sporting trio of enthusiastic and appreciative ladies I have never since handled.") Encouraged by the success of his first trek, Roberts gave himself a company name, Mountain Travel. In 1966, Roberts heard about a fellow in America who'd organized hiking trips for the Sierra Club in South America and the Alps. Leo

LeBon, a Belgian émigré and climbing enthusiast who lived in the San Francisco Bay area, was a branch manager for Thomas Cook and Sons, then the world's largest tour operator. One day, out of the blue, LeBon received a letter from Roberts inquiring if the Sierra Club might be interested in a trek in Nepal. LeBon took the idea to the club's foreign outings committee, which turned thumbs down. (It seems that Roberts wasn't a Sierra Club member.) LeBon then approached higher-ups at Cook with the idea of sponsoring a trek with Roberts. After first refusing to get involved at all, Cook grudgingly agreed to handle just the airline and hotel logistics for such a trip. Recalls LeBon, "They told me, 'As soon as the actual trek starts, you're on your own. We don't know you.'"

LeBon put his own ad in the Sierra Club bulletin. The response was so large—30 people—that two groups had to be formed. LeBon would lead one himself, and he recruited a climbing friend, Barry Bishop, to lead the other. In October, 1967, the 30 trekkers, accompanied by LeBon, Bishop, and Roberts, set off from Pokhara for a leisurely three-week round-trip walk up the Kali Gandaki valley to Jomsom. A fine time was had by all, and the next year LeBon, with Cook's tepid backing, put together four more Roberts-organized treks in Nepal.

It didn't take LeBon long to conclude that this trekking thing might catch on. He worked out an exclusive deal with Roberts, resigned from Thomas Cook, and, along with Bishop and another climbing buddy, Alan Steck, incorporated Mountain Travel U.S. on January 1, 1969. That date is the unofficial birthday of the U.S. adventure travel industry.

That first year, Mountain Travel ran six treks in Nepal, plus one in Kashmir, all operated by Roberts. There were hiking and climbing trips in Corsica, Switzerland, New Zealand, and Kenya as well. By the mid-1970s, Mountain Travel was taking several hundred clients a year to walk in wild places, and word started getting around about this trekking thing. In the late 1970s came a second wave of U.S. trekking companies that included Wilderness Travel and Overseas Adventure Travel. The adventure travel boom was underway.

Meanwhile, in Nepal, a growing number of the tourists, hippies, and wanderers who were flooding into Kathmandu in those days began to venture out into the high country. Trekking services sprouted like mushrooms in Kathmandu, and villagers in the Everest and Annapurna regions began to open "teahouses," very basic trekker accommodations that offered meals. By 1981, 30,000 people a year were trekking in Nepal.

In 1982 Jimmy Roberts sold his trekking business to Tigertops, the jungle lodge in Nepal's Chitwan National Park. After some legal maneuvering, Mountain Travel U.S. kept its name, while Roberts' old company, combined with Tigertops, became Tiger Mountain, under which name it still flourishes today. Mountain Travel U.S. has since merged with whitewater rafting operator Sobek

Unnamed, unclimbed peak, Khumbu region near Mount Everest, Nepal.

Expeditions to become Mountain Travel-Sobek. It, too, is thriving, along with hundreds of other American adventure companies. Leo LeBon, now retired, is still roaming the world at age 67. Jimmy Roberts died in 1997 in Pokhara.

To follow in the footsteps of these trekking pioneers may seem a daunting proposition to the uninitiated. But it's not hard. Virtually any reasonably fit, active, flexible person can do it. Where to begin?

CHOOSING A TREK

The noted jungle trekker Pogo Possum once lamented that he was "confronted with insurmountable opportunities." He might well have been talking about the vast array of treks and trekking outfitters available today. This book winnows the choices down to a more manageable 20 trips and 53 outfitters. But that's still a mind-boggling set of choices.

Start your selection process with the At a Glance section on the second page of each chapter, where the vital statistics for each trek are listed. Categories include:

Trip Length. Total door-to-door time you'll spend away from home.

Time on Trek. Number of days spent on the trail walking.

Walking Distance. Total mileage covered during the trek. In some cases this is estimated.

Maximum Altitude. Highest altitude you'll reach during the trek.

Physical Challenge. The physical demands of each trip are rated 1 through 5, with 1 being the easiest and 5 the hardest. The ratings reflect a combination of altitude, terrain, and daily mileage. Call it the huff-and-puff/sore muscle index.

A 1-rated trek typically involves 4 to 6 hours of daily walking over level terrain at low altitude. Any reasonably active person who is a regular walker could manage a 1-rated trek with little or no pre-trip conditioning. An example is the llama trek in Escalante Canyon that begins on page 146. It's a five-day, 35-mile walk along a riverbed at about 6,000 feet elevation. The one day that involves some ups and downs is optional.

At the other end of the scale, a 5-rated trek would have at least one day of 10 hours or more of walking, daily vertical gains of 4,000 feet or more, and peak altitudes above 17,000 feet. Such a trek would require even energetic young trekkers to embark on some sort of pre-trip fitness program. An example is the Kilimanjaro trek (page 44), which has an 18-hour summit day that includes a climb from 15,000 to 19,000 feet and a descent back to 12,000 feet.

Treks rated 2, 3, or 4—the vast majority of treks in this book—fall somewhere in between, according to altitude, terrain, and daily mileage. We have not listed strict criteria for these factors because different treks have varying combinations of each. But a typical middle-of-the-road 3-rated trek might demand daily walks of 6 to 7 hours, vertical gains and losses of 2,000 to 3,000 feet per day, at altitudes between 10,000 and 15,000 feet. An example of a 3-rated trek is the Inca Trail in Peru (page 102), which runs from 10,000 to 13,000-plus feet, and though averaging only 8 to 10 miles per day, it has some extremely steep sections.

Mental Challenge. A trek challenges the mind as well as the body. Sudden rainstorms, bad roads, stubborn bureaucrats, blisters, smelly toilet pits, and a myriad of other minor unpleasantries

can test a trekker's psychological mettle. Many trips have the potential for serious hazards as well: altitude sickness, nasty disease, dangerous roads, and isolation from help in case of illness or injury. The mental challenge rating quantifies these unpleasantries and hazards. Call it the whine/whimper index.

Because physical exertion plays a big role in one's mental state, the whine/whimper index is closely related to the huff-and-puff/sore muscle rating. In many cases, they are the same. But factors like weather, accommodations, and isolation can raise or drop the mental challenge rating a notch. For example, the Haute Route in

Switzerland (page 120) rates a 3 physically, but only 2 mentally because trekkers stay in well-equipped mountain huts with real beds and meal service. Conversely, the trek to Mount Kailas in Tibet (page 138) rates a 4 physically, but the dreadful five-day jeep ride to the mountain and its extreme isolation and lack of facilities ratchet up the whine/whimper index to 5.

Price Range (independent trek). Includes cost of porters and/or guides hired individually on the spot, plus food and any trail fees. If huts or trekker lodges are available, the number includes the cost of those accommodations.

Price Range (outfitted group trek). The lower number, for a bare-bones trek run by a rock-bottom local operator, typically includes neither hotels before and after the trek, transportation from the staging city, nor side tours. And your guide may not speak much English. The top price is for a deluxe trip by an American outfitter, including hotels, transportation, side tours, and top-notch guides.

Prime Time. Best time of year to take the trek, weather-wise.

Staging City. Where the outfitter typically picks you up to begin the trek. For independent trekkers, the nearest major city or town to the trailhead, where guides and/or local outfitters usually may be found.

Heads Up. Gives notice of possible trouble spots (see page 20).

PHYSICAL FITNESS

Okay, you've sorted out the price, trip length, and prime time to see if they fit your schedule and budget, and rated the physical and mental challenges of the various treks. Now comes the tricky bit: How do you rate yourself? You must be mercilessly objective in rating your own physical fitness. Not how fit you were back in college. Not how fit you could be in a couple of months if you joined a health club. How fit you are now. An accurate self-assessment can spell the difference between the trip of a lifetime and the fiasco of a lifetime.

A sad example: A few years ago I took a trek that included walk-up ascents of both Mount Kenya and Kilimanjaro. The trip had been labeled "strenuous walking, high elevation" in the outfitter's catalog, and the pre-trip material clearly laid out what to expect. Yet two of the group members—a fiftyish sedentary mobile home salesman and a retired newscaster in his late sixties—were physically overmatched from the first day. They struggled on the easier Kenya trek, arriving exhausted and miserable at camp each day, hours behind the rest of us. The trip leader wisely didn't even permit them to begin the much tougher trek up Kilimanjaro. They

Opposite: Children in costume for Gai Jatra festival honoring recently deceased relatives, Kathmandu, Nepal.
Above: Sherpa, Panorama Lodge, Namche, Himalaya.

both had a wretched time, fled for home early, and completely wasted about $6,000—all because they wildly overestimated their own physical fitness.

If you have doubts about your fitness, call an outfitter. But keep in mind that some companies, loath to turn away paying customers, may take an unrealistically upbeat you-can-do-it attitude. (After all, they get to keep your money if you wimp out halfway through.)

In almost all cases—and certainly for any trek rated 3 or higher—a pre-trip workout program of some sort is mandatory. Run, walk, bike, hit the Stairmaster—anything to work the leg muscles and get the heart pumping for at least a half hour—three or four times a week. Tougher treks require tougher pre-trip workouts.

THE ATTITUDE

Assessing your mental fitness for a particular trek takes some serious self-examination as well. Most of us, if prodded, might be willing to admit, "Well, okay, maybe I'm not in as good shape as I should be." But how many among us could bring ourselves to admit, "Yeah, I guess when you get right down to it, I'm a spoiled self-pitying whiner who freaks out at the first hint of a problem."

To enjoy a trek, you gotta have an attitude. The Attitude—the proper spirit of adventure to deal with the vagaries of off-the-beaten-path travel—has a number of facets. It is a cheerful, flexible, easygoing nature and a sense of humor. It's an ability to shrug off—or even relish—minor hardships. It is a certain stoicism in the face of difficulty. A willingness to suck it up and keep

ALTITUDE SICKNESS

Above about 8,000 feet, some trekkers begin to suffer symptoms beyond mere huffing and puffing: headache, nausea, and lethargy. Above 12,000 feet or so, virtually everybody suffers a bit, at least initially. As altitude increases, symptoms can become more severe, including potentially fatal cerebral and pulmonary edema. Oddly, altitude sickness seems to strike almost at random; a vegetarian marathon runner may be laid low while the fat chain-smoking slob in the next tent does just fine. One theory says that susceptibility to altitude sickness depends on one's involuntary background breathing rate, or hypoxic ventilatory response. The higher your rate is, the better. Unfortunately, there's nothing you can do to improve yours; it's a genetic thing.

However, there's a lot you can do to combat altitude sickness in general. The most important thing is to ascend gradually once you get above 10,000 feet or so—ideally, no more than 1,000 feet per day. This gives the body time to acclimatize by building up extra red blood cells and growing more capillaries. Secondly, guzzle water like there's no tomorrow. This helps to keep your blood at the proper level of acidity, which affects your natural breathing rate. Thirdly, take Diamox, a prescription diuretic that has been shown to prevent or delay altitude sickness in most people. And recent studies have shown that the herb ginko biloba can reduce altitude symptoms.

going when you'd rather quit. The ability to adjust quickly when things go wrong—because they almost certainly will go wrong at some point.

The Attitude is personified by the British explorer Wilfrid Thesiger, who spent his life roaming Arabia, Persia, and Africa. Thesiger despised the comforts and security of civilized life. "I long for the chaos, the smells, the untidiness, and the haphazard life," he wrote. "I want color and savagery and hardship. . ." Now it's not actually necessary to *long for* bad smells and hardship as Thesiger did. But a trekker must be able to tolerate them with some measure of good cheer.

I recall a trek in Sikkim in which one middle-aged woman whined incessantly about the food, the weather, the cold, her boots, everything. At night we could hear her in her tent, literally whimpering and moaning. The grand finale came when she claimed to be too tired to walk up a particularly long, steep hill, and demanded that a porter carry her up piggyback. The poor fellow actually did so. Needless to say, she didn't win many friends or have much fun.

Okay, you've narrowed down your selection to a group of treks that meet your price range, schedule, physical abilities, and comfort level. Now what?

Maybe the choice will be easy. Maybe you've always dreamed of seeing the highest point on earth with your own eyes, or watching the sun rise over Machu Picchu. If no place leaps to mind, pick one that has some special significance in your life, however small. Maybe you're a runner, fascinated by those incredibly fit Tarahumara Indians down in Copper Canyon. Maybe you're a confused agnostic looking for divine inspiration on a pilgrimage to Santiago de Compostela, Spain, or Mount Kailas in Tibet. Maybe you're a Hemingway fan who wants to see the real snows of Kilimanjaro.

If you're still undecided, put your list up on the wall and throw a dart at it. Frankly, you can hardly miss. Whether you trek in Nepal, Chile, Mexico, Utah, or Pakistan, you'll be making a long-distance journey by foot through beautiful remote country. You won't have to carry a pack or cook or do the dishes. It doesn't get any better.

OUTFITTED GROUP TREK, OR ON YOUR OWN?

For some treks listed in this book, the question is moot: Individual trekking is either forbidden or logistically improbable. For the rest, you have a decision to make. In almost all cases, the usual tradeoffs apply. Outfitted group trips are more expensive, but relieve you of all logistical chores, which can be substantial in a remote third-world country. You'll meet some good people and feel part of a team. In case of an emergency, you'll have somebody to help. Independent trekking, on the other hand, is cheaper and has the advantages of flexibility and serendipity. Your choice.

In some cases, your choice will depend on where you're going. Nepal, where trekking was essentially invented and the country most trekkers still think of first, is well set up for independent travelers. It's estimated that of the 75,000 trekkers a year who visit Nepal, only about 10 to 20 percent travel with organized groups. Unless you are fluent in Nepali and very resourceful, however, independent trekking in Nepal is limited to the three areas that have

teahouses and other tourist facilities: the Annapurna Circuit, the Everest region, and to a lesser extent, the Langtang area north of Kathmandu.

For many folks, the answer to the outfitter-versus-independent dilemma is simply a matter of money: The outfitted trip is the preferred alternative if you can afford it. Essentially, the group trekker's only logistical responsibility is to call the toll-free number, give them a credit card number, buy the stuff on the equipment list, and show up at the airport on time. You'll save time and hassle, won't get lost, and will have a reasonable assurance that things will turn out pretty much as you expect.

But for some people, that's too easy. These

Thesigeresque souls savor the delight of the unexpected. They enjoy the rewards of blundering their way through, getting lost, asking around, standing in line, struggling to make themselves understood in a strange language, and generally taking responsibility for themselves. If you're that sort of person, by all means, do it yourself.

For other people, the fatal drawback of group treks is the group. Spending a lot of time in close quarters with five, ten, or fifteen strangers is not everyone's cup of tea. They simply don't want to risk the possibility of getting stuck with some pain in the ass for three weeks.

But one man's "pain in the ass" is another man's "idiosyncratic personality that can easily be ignored." In my experience, the pain-in-the-ass-quotient on group treks is surprisingly low, and more than offset by the likelihood of meeting some absolutely splendid people. Trekking groups seems to self-select out most of the whiners. In the two dozen or so group adventure trips I've taken, I can recall only one true psycho (the piggyback woman), maybe three moderately annoying jerks, a modicum of bores, an overwhelming majority of fine folks, and 15 or 20 soul mates. After one trek, five of the seven group members showed up at my house a year later for a reunion party (one guy came from Australia). Twelve years

later, I'm still in touch with all of them. Friends like that are worth the occasional jerk.

If you absolutely can't stand other people, yet don't want the logistical hassles of doing a trip on your own, there is a third possibility: a custom trip just for you (and maybe your family or friends) from an established outfitter. Bring your wallet.

CHOOSING AN OUTFITTER

Okay, you've finished the fun part, figuring out where to go.

If you've decided to travel with an outfitter, now comes the not-so-fun part: choosing one.

Most of the treks in this book are served by multiple outfitters, which are listed in alphabetical order. (We've made no attempt to rate outfitters, a virtually impossible task that, to do fairly, would require years of research and a budget of several hundred thousand dollars.) In the absence of star-ratings, we can state with some assurance that each outfitter listed here is a competent, established company. Each has its own strengths, weaknesses, and style that may or may not be a good fit for you. It's up to you to sort them out for yourself.

There are three basic kinds of trekking outfitters listed. The first is the full-service U.S. company that creates its own itineraries, sends

Opposite: Torres del Paine National Park, Chile. Above: Novice monk, Enchey Monastery, Gangtok, Sikkim, India.

along its own trip leaders, and closely supervises the local people who operate the trek. These outfitters set quality standards and take full responsibility for their product. Essentially they "own" their treks. The "Big Three" of these full-service trekking companies are Mountain Travel-Sobek, Wilderness Travel, and Geographic Expedi-tions. Typically, their prices are at the top end of the scale.

A second tier of American outfitters are really just booking agents for treks run by overseas companies. The American agents choose these local operators carefully, but they basically just sell the trips and send you the paperwork.

Their sales people won't know much about the treks beyond what's in the brochure. Among the major American trek-booking agents are Adventure Center, Himalayan Travel, and Safari-centre. Their prices are typically 20 to 50 percent below the upper-tier outfitters mentioned above, due partly to lower overhead, and partly to the fewer frills philosophy typical of the overseas outfitters they represent.

The third category is the foreign trek operators themselves. Until recently, dealing directly with overseas companies from the United States was frustrating, slow, and expensive, but the Internet has changed all that. Basic trek info is a

TROUBLE SPOTS

Many treks take place in remote third-world countries, where the politics sometimes turn dicey. Border squabbles, clan warfare, religious strife, and just plain banditry can flare up unpredictably in areas where treks take place. For example, as this book was being written, the Indians and Pakistanis were shooting at each other in Kargil, about 50 miles from the trekking route described on page 90, and Uganda was embroiled in the Congolese civil war, temporarily shutting down the Ruwenzori trek route described on page 82.

Of course by the time these words appear in print—our publishing lead time is roughly a year—these areas may well be perfectly safe. On the other hand, new trouble spots may have flared up as well. The bottom line: we can offer no specific advice on political trouble spots in these pages; the situations change too fast. It's up to you to check things out yourself before

you go. Those trouble spots we're aware of will be mentioned in the At a Glance section under Heads Up.

If you're trekking with a reputable American outfitter, there is little to worry about. Outfitters closely monitor the countries where they run treks, and will typically cancel a trip if they feel there is even a slight risk of danger (dead clients are very bad PR). If you're trekking on your own, call an outfitter or two that run treks in the same area. You might also check the State Department's travelers' warnings (202-647-5225; www.travel.state.gov/travel warnings.), although these tend to have an ultra-conservative the-sky-is-falling take, designed as they are for the average timid tourist who wants an iron-clad guarantee of absolute safety under all conditions. As a trekker, of course, you are made of sterner stuff.

mouse-click away, and international phone rates are getting cheaper every day. In most cases, we've listed only a few local operators, but you'll find many more when you arrive in trekking hotbeds like Kathmandu and Cuzco. There are plenty of competent local outfitters, but plenty of

marginal and even incompetent ones as well. You can save a lot of money with an in-country outfitter, but you can also get burned. Y'all be careful, now, hear?

Armed with this basic understanding of whom you're dealing with, you're now ready to

Tekes River Valley, Tian Shan foothills, eastern Kazakhstan.

start the outfitter selection process.

The first thing you'll notice is that various outfitters offer what is ostensibly the same trek at wildly diverse prices. Is somebody trying to rip you off? Probably not. The fact is, the wildly diverse prices almost invariably reflect wildly diverse levels of service, from no-frills to frills-out-the-wazoo. Usually, you get what you pay for.

Your goal is to find the outfitter with precisely the frills you're willing to pay for—no more, no less. Here's how:

Ask for a Catalog. Promotional materials from outfitters run the gamut from typewritten screeds to huge glossy volumes that would sit nicely on a Park Avenue coffee table. You can't judge a company solely by its catalog, of course, but it does give a feel for it. Mom and Pop, or slick and corporate? Adventure supermarket, or treks only? Worldwide, or a one-country specialist?

Get a detailed day-to-day itinerary for the trek you're interested in. Compare it carefully with the itineraries of other outfitters. Look for differences in routing, accommodations, rest days, side tours, and so forth.

Once you've made the first cut of outfitters based on their printed material:

Get on the phone and start asking questions. How long have you run this trek? Do you operate the trip yourself, or use a local operator? How long have you worked with the operator? What's your cancellation/refund policy?

Blitz the outfitter with questions about the trip leader. Some of my best trek memories are the leaders, among them the widow of Everest summitter Tenzing Norgay, and a former Mexican revolutionary street fighter. The trip leader will be your guide/interpreter/mother hen/drill sergeant/group psychologist. Ask the outfitter: How long has the trip leader worked for you? How much experience does he have in this country? On this trek? Any special knowledge about the local people, geology, or wildlife? Ask for the trip leader's phone number and call him for a little chat. Nothing heavy, just get a feel for this person's style, and how the two of you relate.

A trip leader can make or break your trip. For example, a few years ago I took a Nepal trek with an easygoing American trip leader, a Nepal veteran who took great delight in sharing his inti-mate knowledge of the place with us. After dinner each night, he would read aloud from Eric Newby's hilarious classic, *A Short Walk in the Hindu Kush,* a chapter a night for 20 nights. We had a marvelous time. Two years later, my sister took the same trek, with the same company. Different trip leader, though—a Nepali fellow who, although he managed the trek efficiently, spoke virtually no English. "I felt like I was in a vacuum," my sister reported. She had a lousy time.

Ask the outfitter for phone numbers of former clients for this trek. A good outfitter will be happy to pass along this information. Call them all (don't be shy; people love to talk about their trips.) A savvy outfitter won't give you the names of any unhappy customers, so you may have to read between the lines. Does the client rave about the trip or just endorse it? Does this person seem to share your priorities about what makes a good trip?

This second round of inquiry should winnow the outfitters down to a short list that match your needs and karma pretty closely. Now it's crunch time: How much are you willing to pay?

ANATOMY OF TREK EXPENSES

A trek can be surprisingly expensive. I can still recall the astonishment in my friends' eyes a few years back when I told them about my trek in

Opposite: Porter near Gangtok, Sikkim, India. Above: Mountain Travel's original catalog; the trekking company was founded in January 1969, marking the birth of organized adventure travel in the U. S.

Africa. Alas, it was not my rhapsodic accounts of sunrise from the summit of Kilimanjaro that so amazed them. It was the cost of the trip: $3,890 for 19 days. "Are you kidding?" asked one friend, incredulous. "You spent $200 a night to sleep on the ground and eat beans?"

Not exactly. But the cost of trekking can be surprisingly high, on par with the daily cost of staying in a four-star hotel. Where does all the money go?

Let's look at an example: the classic 30-day Annapurna circuit trek in Nepal, offered by a number of outfitters at prices ranging from $1,380 to $3,090. The 224 percent price variation among the various outfitters makes it a superb specimen for economic analysis and a litmus test for just exactly where each outfitter puts its priorities.

Broken out below are the various costs of the Annapurna circuit trek operated by Geo-graphic Expeditions (GeoEx), a big San Francisco outfitter that charges $2,690, in the upper-middle of the price spectrum. The trip runs at that price with anywhere from 6 to 16 trekkers. (Some outfitters use "tier-pricing," adding surcharges for smaller groups. Mountain Travel-Sobek, for example, prices its Annapurna trip at a base cost of $2,790 for groups of 10 to 15, but adds $300 a head for groups of 5 to 9.) The cost-per-person numbers for the Geographic Expeditions trip broken out on the following pages are based on a group size of 10, the point at which the trip begins to make a profit.

Here's where Geographic Expeditions puts its money—and its priorities—on the Annapurna circuit:

FIELD EXPENSES

Field expenses include camping expenses, plus hotels, transportation, and everything that GeoEx

TREKKING POLES

You can always tell when a German trekking group is approaching. Everybody has trekking poles, giving the procession the look of a giant centipede. My first reaction to this phenomenon was a snort of derision. Wimps! Even worse, high-tech trendy wimps.

But then, out of curiosity, I borrowed a pair for a day. Hmmm. They sure made steep descents a lot easier. And, well, yes, they seemed to take a bit of load off my legs during steep climbs. And, yeah, those creek crossings were a piece of cake. I caved in and bought a pair for my most recent trek, in Kazakhstan. After ten days of walking, I judged them redundant (or even slightly burdensome) on moderate sections of trail. But the steeper the ascent (either up or down), the more useful they became. Over three steep passes on rough trails, they were virtually indispensable for my 52-year-old legs. Would I recommend them? *Jawohl.*

If you do buy a pair of trekking poles, make sure they're adjustable. (Different lengths are best for climbing and descending.) Prices typically run $50 to $100 a pair.

pays out of pocket to run the trek, as detailed here.

Hotels in Kathmandu: $264. GeoEx includes four nights at the top-drawer Shangri-La, renowned for its courtyard gardens. Cut-rate outfitters can shave costs here. For example, the British outfitter Explore (represented in the United States by Adventure Center) puts up its clients at the quite decent—but far from luxurious—Yellow Pagoda, near Kathmandu's funky Thamel district. Cost: around $20 a night per person. That's one reason Explore's Annapurna trek comes in at $1,555, 42 percent below Geographic Expeditions.

At the other extreme, Mountain Travel-Sobek, whose Annapurna trek is the dearest of the lot, puts up its people at the Yak and Yeti, a five-star $150-a-night palace. Take your pick.

Sightseeing in Kathmandu: $25. Two half-day van tours with guides. Virtually all outfitters provide local tours; not much room to squeeze costs here.

Transportation: $211. Most outfitters bus their clients between Kathmandu and Pokhara, the jumping-off spot for Annapurna. GeoEx flies, a semi-extravagance that costs $193. Airport van transfers at both ends add $18.

Trek permits and fees: $55. Mandatory.

Medical evacuation insurance: $96. GeoEx is the only company to include automatic medevac coverage in its standard trip price. This is a good deal for clients; such a policy purchased individually would typically cost about 5 percent of the trip cost, or roughly $135 in the case of the GeoEx Annapurna trek.

Duffel bag: $39. GeoEx magnanimously gives each trekker a sturdy duffel bag to carry gear. Of course they don't really "give" it to you, but the $39 cost built in to the trek price is a good deal for a bag that would retail in the $75 to $100 range.

Contingency fund: $21. A kitty for the unforeseen: meals while waiting for a weather-delayed flight, inflated kerosene prices due to a local shortage, complimentary beers along the trail if the trip leader is in a good mood, and so forth.

Trip leader's salary: $11. In a major cost-cutting move, GeoEx uses a Nepalese Sherpa trip leader, or sirdar, who earns about $8 per day. (Rather a handsome salary, actually, in a country where the average per capita income is perhaps $300 a year.) The sirdar's prime concern is getting you from A to B safely and keeping the trek staff cracking. He will probably not have the time—nor the education, language skills, or cross-cultural deftness—to regale you with stories or lectures on local history, geology and wildlife.

A Western trip leader, hired in addition to the sirdar and typically paid $100 to $125 a day to schmooze and educate the customers full time, would increase the price of the GeoEx Annapurna trip by $460 per person. A third alternative, a Western-educated Sherpa schmoozer/leader who would hang out with the clients while the sirdar took care of logistics, would earn about

Mackinnon Pass, Milford Track, South Island, New Zealand.

$75 a day and add about $350 to the trip price.

GeoEx's philosophy is that on well-trodden classic routes like Annapurna, where plenty of maps and guidebooks are available, a Western trip leader is not so necessary. "Our clients prefer the more economical approach," says Jim Sano of GeoEx.

Sherpa trek staff: $111. Salaries of camp helpers and cooks—ranging from $4 to $6 per day—are pretty standard. No place to cut fat here.

Porters: $522. Anywhere from 30 to 40 porters are required for the Annapurna circuit, at a standard rate of about $4 per day. GeoEx hires extra porters to carry out trash, and also provides insurance for porters at a cost of $25 per trekker.

Camping equipment: $80. GeoEx amortizes its sleeping tents, mess and toilet tents, kitchen equipment, and medical equipment over three years. Unlike most outfitters, it also provides sleeping bags.

Food: $258. This figure includes all meals on the trek. Lunches and dinners in Kathmandu and Pokhara are not included. The trekker pays for those on his own.

Kerosene: $111. Approximately 200 gallons of kerosene, at about $5 a gallon, are used for cooking, heating wash water, and boiling drinking water. (Extra porters are required to carry the fuel, of course.) Burning wood is not permitted on Annapurna treks due to deforestation problems.

Total camping expenses for the 24 days on the trail—camp staff, camping equipment, food, kerosene, and porters—amount to $1093 per person, about $45 per day.

Some outfitters dispense with camping altogether and put their people up in teahouses, very basic lodgings along the route where room and board typically run $10 to $15 per day. Teahouse treks require no camping equipment, staff, food, or kerosene, and the number of porters required for the trek falls from about 40 to 15. Exodus, another British outfitter, operates its Annapurna circuit as a teahouse trek—a major reason it charges the rock-bottom price of $1,380.

The downside of teahouses is smoke, bedbugs, lack of privacy, unpredictable sanitation, and too-predictable food. "It's virtually impossible for a Westerner to eat in teahouses for three weeks without getting sick," advises one veteran Himalaya guide. "And you get pretty tired of *dahl baat* (beans and rice) after a while." Most teahouses use at least some wood for fuel, so teahouse trekkers contribute indirectly to local deforestation.

Total field expenses. For the GeoEx Annapurna trip, total field expenses come to $1,804 per trekker.

OVERHEAD EXPENSES

But of course the trip price must also cover the mundane overhead that figures into the price of everything from paper clips to B-2 stealth bombers. Here's how GeoEx figures its overhead for the Annapurna trek:

Home office (Rent, utilities, toll-free phone, etc.): $158. GeoEx's San Francisco headquarters is a beautifully refurbished Victorian house in the heart of a very expensive city. Smaller, leaner outfits can easily undercut them here.

Kathmandu office: $55. An old house in a modest district. Not much to cut here.

Headquarters staff salaries: $247. GeoEx, along with other top-dollar outfitters, provides lavish pre-trip customer service—reams of medical advice, help with visas, toll-free phone consultations, etc. This requires a lot of well-trained people in a high-priced job market. Less service-oriented outfitters in smaller towns can easily undercut GeoEx in this category.

Marketing: $86. This is quite a modest figure, actually—primarily because GeoEx does a

Namche Bazaar, the point of departure for treks into the Everest region of the Himalaya.

lot of corporate business, which inherently gets more marketing bang per buck. Other big outfitters typically have marketing costs of about $150 to $200 per trekker. GeoEx spends a total of about $50,000 a year to produce its plush, cleverly written catalog, and at least that much more in postage to mail it out. Some outfitters spend more than $300,000 a year on their catalogs—better than $100 per person.

Commissions: $118. A quarter of GeoEx clients book through travel agents, who skim 10 percent off the top. Three-quarters pay with credit cards, which take an additional 2 to 5 percent. Not all outfitters follow suit; Overseas Adventure Travel does not accept credit cards (except for initial deposits) and by not pursuing travel agent business manages to pay commission on less than 10 percent of its business.

Total overhead expenses. For the GeoEx Annapurna trip, total overhead expenses come to $664 per trekker.

THE BOTTOM LINE

Add it all up—field expenses plus overhead—and it costs GeoEx $2,468 to take you around Annapurna. That leaves $222 from your $2,690 payment, an 8.3 percent profit margin. This profit-per-trekker number would increase by about five percentage points—roughly $135—with each additional trip member, and disappear altogether with eight or fewer.

The bottom line on Geographic Expeditions' priorities on the Annapurna trek: good customer service, a nice hotel in Kathmandu, a flight to Pokhara, top-notch medical and insurance protection, a "free" duffel bag—but no Western leader. If those are your priorities, too, then you've got a perfect match: go with Geographic. But if you have different priorities, check to see where the other outfitters put their money. The bottom line, after all, is the bottom line.

GETTING READY

This section won't tell you how to apply for a passport, or remind you to have a neighbor collect your mail while you're away. You know that stuff already. That's Traveling 101. But a trek, especially one in a far-off third-world country, demands more than undergraduate planning skills. Arcane matters like helicopter evacuation insurance, State Department warnings of guerrilla activity, malaria pills, and moisture-wicking underwear can loom large and confusing to the uninitiated.

For independent trekkers, a guidebook is a must. Check the Recommended Reading section of each trek chapter for a list of recommended guidebooks. It wouldn't hurt group trekkers to get a guidebook, either, just to get a feel for the trek and make sure you don't miss any good stuff along the way. Our favorite place to buy guidebooks, as well as the other books on our recommended reading list, is AdventurousTraveler.com (800-282-3963).

But the group trekker's primary resource is the outfitter. The better companies put a lot of effort into their pre-trip info packets. Your outfitter has probably taken several hundred clients on this particular trek, and the info pack is a distillation of everything they've learned. It

Tian Shan Range, Uzbekistan.

sounds laughably obvious, but the single most important thing you can do to prepare for a trek is to follow the outfitter's recommendations to the letter. They know what works. Listen to them.

Astonishingly and inexplicably, vast legions of trekkers fail to do so. Jim Traverso, a former guide for Overseas Adventure Travel, recalls a trekking client who showed up in Kathmandu without hiking boots. She claimed the pre-trip equipment list hadn't really emphasized them. In fact, as Traverso patiently pointed out to her, the equipment list for that particular trip began with the words "The single most important item you'll bring along on your trek is your hiking boots. . . ."

Added Traverso wearily, "Every day I would get calls from clients asking, 'Do I really need. . . ?' Every time, my answer was, 'Yes, you really need....'"

In addition to recommended clothing and equipment, your outfitter will tell you all about visas, health requirements, insurance options, sun protection, and other nuts and bolts. But here are some tips your outfitter may not have thought of.

Ziploc bags. Clear plastic bags are invaluable for storing items that must stay dry, isolating clothes that are wet and/or dirty, and just generally organizing your stuff into small, manageable, and clearly visible compartments.

Mini-tape recorder. Everybody brings home photos, but think what your friends will say when you bring home audio memories instead: kids laughing, the porters singing around the campfire, philosophical musings along the trail.

Pee bottle. The average trekking client is 50 years old, the age when bladder capacity begins to shrink, especially in men. Assuming you have an understanding tent-mate, a wide-mouth plastic bottle will save a bone-chilling midnight trip to the latrine. Women's models are also available.

Small toys to entertain local kids. Frisbees, Wiffle balls, finger puppets and wind-up toys are great icebreakers. A guy on a Nepal trek with me a few years ago was an instant hero in every village we passed through by virtue of a hackey-sack. The kids went wild.

Personal journal. Trekking trips, because they remove you so completely from your everyday life, invariably stimulate self-reflection and musing. Should I quit my boring job when I get back home? Does it really matter who wins the World Series? Does this guy Buddha really have

the secret to life and death? Write this stuff down. Years from now, you'll be amazed at what went through your head.

And one final thought before you head for the airport. Many Americans are surprised at the intelligence, sensitivity, and sophistication of so-called "primitive" third world people. Our old friend Wilfrid Thesiger, writing of the Arabian nomads with whom he traveled, wrote, "I went there with a belief in my own racial superiority, but in their tents I felt like an uncouth, inarticulate barbarian, an intruder from a shoddy and materialistic society." You may not go to Thesiger's extreme, but smug preconceptions about the inferiority of "primitive" people will shut you off from what, in the long run, often turns out to be the greatest reward of trekking: not the mountains, but the people.

Opposite: Tibetan Buddhist Lamas, Mani Rimdu festival, Tengboche Monastery, Khumbu, Himalaya, Nepal.
Overleaf: On the high plateau, Grand Staircase-Escalante National Monument, southern Utah.

Gokyo & Everest Base Camp

If you could only take one trek in your life...

As you head out on the trail from the Sherpa village of Namche Bazaar toward Everest, thereby commencing the most storied trek in the world, you will be tracing the footsteps of the 20th century's two greatest mountain explorers: H. W. Tilman and Eric Shipton. These two pipe-smoking British gentlemen, friends and regular expedition-mates, spent their lives filling in blank spaces on maps—especially in the Himalayas. On separate expeditions in 1950 and 1951, Tilman's and Shipton's groups were the first Westerners to set foot in the Everest region of Nepal, known as Khumbu. Tilman called it "the grandest 30 miles of the Himalayas," and the walk from Namche Bazaar to what is now Everest Base Camp remains for many people the ultimate trek, the trek you would choose if, God forbid, you could only make one in your life.

Nepal was closed to foreigners for most of

Sherpa yak drivers enjoy rancid yak butter tea break, Dzongla Meadows, Khumbu Region, Nepal.

the first half of the 20th century. (The 1933 and 1938 Tilman/Shipton expeditions to Everest, as well as the earlier expeditions of George Mallory, had approached the mountain—whose summit lies on the border between Tibet and Nepal—from the Tibetan, or north side.) But the Nepali authorities began to loosen up a bit by the late 1940s, allowing a Tilman expedition to explore Langtang and Annapurna. But all British requests to visit the Everest region were denied, a bitter blow to both Tilman and Shipton, who had employed many Sherpas on their expeditions all over Asia, and heard the wondrous tales they told of their homeland in the shadow of Everest. Shipton later wrote, "For 20 years, ever since I had first known the Sherpas, I had longed, above all else, to visit their homeland."

But it was Tilman who got lucky first. Loitering at a British Embassy reception in Kathmandu after his Annapurna expedition, Tilman ran into the father of an old American climbing companion, Charles Houston, who casually mentioned that he'd gotten permission for a trek to Everest, and would Tilman like to come along? Echoing Shipton, Tilman had long considered the Everest region of Nepal to be "my humble Mecca." He accepted immediately.

After 16 days of hard trekking from the Indian border, on November 14, 1950 the party walked into Namche Bazaar, the first Westerners ever to do so. They were immediately mobbed by astonished villagers, who had to be shooed away by the headman. A few who had previously served as porters on British expeditions were allowed to remain. They were the only locals, Tilman wrote, "considered to be sufficiently well disciplined to refrain from laughing at our strange ways and stranger faces."

Tilman and Houston left immediately for the long-awaited close-up look at the south side of Everest. They stopped first at Tengboche Monastery, on a grassy saddle overlooking two great rivers and flanked by four of the six highest mountains in the world. "It would be difficult to imagine, much less find, a finer site for worship or meditation," Tilman wrote. "Lamas may laugh at our love for climbing mountains, but undoubtedly they themselves take great delight in looking at them." They stayed at the monastery overnight,

AT A GLANCE

TRIP LENGTH	27–30 days	PRICE RANGE (INDEPENDENT TREK)	$600–$1,000
TIME ON TREK	18–22 days	PRICE RANGE (OUTFITTED GROUP TREK)	
WALKING DISTANCE	130 miles	$1,500–$3,000	
MAXIMUM ALTITUDE	18,200 feet	PRIME TIME	October–November, April–May
PHYSICAL CHALLENGE	1 2 3 4 ⑤	STAGING CITY	Kathmandu, Nepal
MENTAL CHALLENGE	1 2 3 4 ⑤		

much impressed by the hospitality of their hosts. "We found they had the pleasant custom of fortifying their guests with a snorter before breakfast," Tilman noted approvingly.

They continued up the Imja Khola River toward Everest, hoping to see a possible route to

Saturday market at the Sherpa village of Namche Bazaar, gateway to Everest.

the summit. But even well up along the Khumbu Glacier, which tumbled down from Everest, the lower slopes of the mountain lay frustratingly out of sight behind a shoulder of Nuptse, a neighboring peak. Hoping to get a better view of Everest's South Ridge and the Western Cwm—the steep valley above the Khumbu Glacier that Tilman and Shipton had glimpsed in 1935 from the Tibetan side—Tilman and Houston climbed "a subsidiary feature of about 18,000 feet. . .a little hummock" on the west side of the Khumbu Glacier. That "little hummock" was Kala Pattar, today renowned among Everest trekkers as perhaps the finest viewpoint for the world's highest mountain.

Frustratingly, even from Kala Pattar, it was impossible to see the Western Cwm or South Ridge. Though Everest's upper terrain appeared forbidding indeed, Tilman concluded hopefully that "one cannot rule out the possibility of there

being a route to the summit by the south ridge." Pressed for time, Tilman and Houston returned to Namche Bazaar, and then back across the border to India.

In 1951, no doubt titillated by Tilman's peek at Everest's south side, Shipton led an expedition back to Khumbu with the express purpose of scouting a climbing route up the Khumbu Glacier and the as-yet-unseen Western Cwm above it. "I put the odds against our finding a practicable route at about 30 to 1," Shipton later wrote.

As was Shipton's style, the expedition was small, only four people. But at the last moment, Shipton agreed to allow a couple of unknown young New Zealand climbers, already in the Himalayas, to join up with his group along the trail. One of the Kiwis was a tall, robust fellow, a beekeeper by trade, named Edmund Hillary. In awe of the legendary Shipton, Hillary nervously anticipated their rendezvous. "Eric Shipton came forward to greet us," Hillary later recalled, "and I felt a sense of relief at his unshaven face and scruffy clothes. I have rarely seen a more disreputable bunch, and my visions of changing for dinner faded away forever."

Approaching Namche Bazaar, the group received a tumultuous welcome. "At each village along the path, all the Sherpa inhabitants. . . turned out to greet us, and we were invited, often dragged, into one of the houses for a session of chang-drinking," wrote Shipton. "I met scores of friends from pre-war expeditions. . . . After a while I found it increasingly difficult to recognize anyone, and I marched along in a happy alcoholic haze."

Mount Everest viewed from Khumbu Glacier. Tilman had glimpsed Everest from near Khumbu in 1932; Shipton returned in 1951, and, with young Edmund Hillary, first beheld a feasible way to climb Everest.

Once in Namche, the trekkers joined in a huge all-night village party that featured intricate dancing. "Our participation. . .produced. . . wild hilarity," wrote Shipton. "Our inept caperings were greeted with roars of hysterical laughter from the great gathering of villagers. Certainly the sight of Ed, tall and long-limbed, supported between two stocky Sherpa wenches, an expression of powerful concentration on his face, would have diverted a much more sophisticated audience."

Following Tilman's route, Shipton proceeded to Tengboche (he found it "enchanting") and on into the heart of Khumbu, the promised land that he had dreamed of seeing for 20 years. "The reality was even lovelier than the dream," Shipton exulted. Once encamped on the Khumbu Glacier, Shipton and Hillary, hoping to finally get a glimpse of the Western Cwm, climbed a ridge above Kala Pattar to an altitude

Nepalese home, Thame Village, west of Namche Bazaar at an elevation of about 11,000 feet.

Trekking to Thame Village, a side hike from Namche Bazaar.

of about 20,000 feet. The extra 2,000 feet made all the difference. "There before us was the head of the Western Cwm. . .and the slopes leading to the South Col. . .we realized at once that there was a perfectly feasible route from the Cwm to the Col. This was a momentous discovery, for this was the main object of our quest."

In fact, Shipton and Hillary's first look into the Western Cwm could be considered the key moment in the history of Everest, the moment when the two men most closely linked to the mountain's past and future first realized that the mountain could be climbed. It happened virtually within shouting distance of a place visited by hundreds, if not thousands, of trekkers every year.

THE ROUTE

The standard out-and-back route from Namche Bazaar to Everest Base Camp sees up to 10,000 trekkers a year. The more roundabout route we have selected here, via the Dudh Kosi Valley and a high pass called Cho La, is far less crowded, longer, a bit more challenging, and includes the beautiful Gokyo area. This route is referred to by some outfitters as the "Ultimate Everest" trek.

You'll start in Kathmandu with a Twin Otter flight to the aircraft-carrier-like airstrip at Lukla, where the trek begins. In a couple of days, you'll reach Namche Bazaar then head on up the Dudh Kosi valley to Tengboche Monastery. At Tengboche, the main route toward Everest Base Camp winds up the Imja Khola River, but you'll stay to the west in the Dudh Kosi valley and continue to Gokyo, with 26,900-foot Cho Oyu looming ahead. You'll then head east across a 17,800-foot snow-covered pass, Cho La, before descending to rejoin the main trekking route. Then you'll continue north along the Khumbu Glacier to Everest Base Camp, just below the famed Khumbu Icefall. You'll then follow the main route back to Lukla via Pheriche, Pangboche (site of another monastery), Tengboche, and Namche Bazaar.

The route can also be done in reverse, crossing Cho La in a westerly direction.

Most trekkers spend several days making side hikes to monasteries and viewpoints such as Thame, Gokyo Ri, Kala Pattar, and Chhukung Ridge. Any itinerary should also include a number of rest days for altitude acclimatization.

WHAT TO EXPECT

This is a challenging high-altitude trek that will put you as deep into the heart of the world's highest mountains as it's possible to go without crampons and technical climbing skills. The local Sherpa people, though heavily influenced by Western values—Sherpa teenagers wearing Patagonia, Nike, and Vuarnet far outnumber the Buddhist monks at Tengboche, and yes, there's a

YETI OR NOT?

During their wide-ranging Himalayan travels, both Tilman and Shipton reported seeing mysterious footprints in the snow. Both seemed willing to believe the claims of their Sherpa companions that the footprints were made by yetis, or abominable snowmen, the mysterious hairy manlike creatures that were reputed to roam the Himalayas.

The most famous and well-documented yeti footprints of all were discovered by Shipton on his 1951 expedition into the Khumbu. Years later, he recalled, "At a height of about 19,000 feet, late one afternoon, we came across those curious footprints in the snow, the report of which has caused a certain amount of public interest in Britain. We did not follow them further than was convenient, a mile or so, for we were carrying heavy loads at the time....I have in the past found many sets of these curious footprints, and have tried to follow them, but have always lost them in the moraine or rocks at the side of the glacier. These particular ones seemed to be very fresh, probably not more than 24 hours old. Sen Tensing, who had no doubt that the creatures (for there had been at least two) that had made the tracks were 'Yetis' or wild men, told me that

two years before, he and a number of other Sherpas had seen one of them at a distance of about 25 yards at Tengboche. He described it as half man and half beast, standing about five feet six inches, with a tall pointed head, its body covered with reddish brown hair, but with a hairless face."

Tilman saw no yeti tracks during his 1950 Everest trip, but there was no lack of conversation about the creatures among the Sherpas he met along the way. "As we sat in the secure circle of the fire, our backs to the stone wall of the hut, the talk naturally turned to the Abominable Snowman. As one might expect they are found in numbers, especially around Namche Bazaar in the depths of winter when the cold drives them lower. Danu affirmed that the previous year a friend of his named Lakhpa Tensing had had his face so badly mauled by one, on the Nangpa La, that he died. By running downhill, which of course is the only way a man can run at these heights, one can usually get away from these creatures whose long hair, falling over their eyes, hampers them; but the unfortunate Lakhpa had apparently tripped and lying half-stunned by the fall became an easy prey."

Top: The 1951 team, with Shipton (left, standing) and Hillary (right, seated). Above: Shipton's photograph of a yeti footprint, with ice ax head for scale.

disco in Namche Bazaar—have for the most part retained the deep spirituality and good cheer amid heart-wrenching poverty that have won the hearts of so many Western trekkers.

Altitude acclimatization should be taken very seriously on this trek; you'll spend a week above 15,000 feet. Take several rest days for acclimatization on the way up, and guzzle water like there's no tomorrow. (The prescription drug Diamox can help, too.)

On an outfitted trek, you'll be treated to the highest standard of trekking amenities in the world—trekking was invented here, after all—with steaming cups of tea handed through your tent flap as your wake-up call each morning. Independent trekkers typically stay in teahouses, modest hotels along the trail. From Lukla to Namche Bazaar, the teahouses are quite nice, with private rooms usually available. Above Namche Bazaar, there are primarily dormitory-style accommodations.

GUIDES AND OUTFITTERS

No other trek in this book offers such a plethora of choices. You can spend anywhere from $10 a day to $125 a day for a Base Camp-Gokyo trek (not including visa and trek permit fees, which typically run $3 to $5 per day). Starting at the bottom of the scale, here are the various options:

$10/day: Independent economy teahouse trek. No porter or guide; room and board at the cheapest teahouses. High tolerance for exotic bacteria, smoke, and bedbugs recommended.

$20/day: Guide and/or porter-assisted upscale independent teahouse trek. Better food and lodging, plus a guide and/or porter to show you the way, help carry your stuff, and help arrange accommodations each night. And, if you pass through the guide's home village, you'll almost certainly be invited in for dinner and a cup or three of *chang,* the local beer.

There are two major caveats for independent trekkers on our Gokyo-Base Camp route, however. The first is the difficulty of getting flights to (and especially back from) Lukla during the peak trekking season. Even if you do manage to get a reservation, flights often get cancelled by weather, resulting in backups of hundreds of passengers and mad scrambles for the few available seats when the weather clears. Group trekkers usually have the advantage in these free-for-alls because their trek leaders can bring influence to bear on ticket agents. The second caveat is that there are no hotels or teahouses along the most remote segment of the route, from Gokyo over the Cho La to Lobuje. This means you'll have to pitch a tent for at least one night and carry your own food.

LOCAL OUTFITTERS

$40-$60/day: Group trek with Nepalese outfitter. In Kathmandu there are at least 150 licensed trekking operators who can take you to Gokyo and Everest Base Camp. It's also possible to sign up for group treks in Lukla. We'll make no attempt to list Nepalese outfitters here; there are just too many of them. When selecting an outfitter in Kathmandu, simply use the same careful consumer skills you'd use back home for

Opposite: Sherpa woman turning giant prayer wheel, Namche Bazaar.
Above: Moon over Everest, Lhotse, and Makalu at sunset taken from Gokyo Ri (17,520 feet).

Rice terracing in Nepal. Much of the trekking around Everest is at lower, more lush elevations.

any major purchase: Ask a lot of questions and go with your gut feel for the people you meet. Generally, it's a good idea to choose an outfitter recommended by some trusted source—a contact back home, another trekker you meet in Nepal, the Nepal Department of Tourism, or the Trekking Agents Association of Nepal. Also check the Visit Nepal Network (011-977-1-416239, www.visitnepal.com)

On second thought, we'll list one Nepalese trekking operator—the company that in effect invented trekking, founded in 1964 by the legendary Col. Jimmy Roberts, a British Army officer who spent much of his career in Southeast Asia and eventually retired in Nepal.

MOUNTAIN TRAVEL NEPAL
011- 977-1-411225
www.tigermountain.com/Trekking/MTN.htm
$1,900 for 18 days

U.S. OUTFITTERS

$75-$125/day: Full-service group trek with U.S. operator. Includes hotels in staging city, transportation to and from trailheads, Western trip leader (usually), and side tours in Kathmandu.

ADVENTURE CENTER
800-227-8747
www.adventure-center.com
$1,799 for 22 days

CAMP 5 EXPEDITIONS
800-914-3834
www.camp5.com
$2,295 for 22 days

GEOGRAPHIC EXPEDITIONS
800-777-8183
www.geoex.com
$2,295 for 27 days

HIMALAYAN HIGH TREKS
800-455-8735
www.HimalayanHighTreks.com
$2,000 for 29 days

HIMALAYAN TRAVEL
800-225-2380
www.govp.com/himtravel.htm
$2,650 for 25 days

KE ADVENTURE TRAVEL
800-497-9675
www.keadventure.com
$2,495 for 20 days

MOUNTAIN TRAVEL-SOBEK
888-687-6235
www.mtsobek.com
$2,790 for 29 days

SNOW LION EXPEDITIONS
800-525-8735
www.snowlion.com
$2,900 for 22 days

WILDERNESS TRAVEL
800-800-368-2794
www.wildernesstravel.com
$2,295 for 27 days

RECOMMENDED READING

■ *NEPAL HIMALAYA*, H. W. Tilman The famed explorer's account of his travels in Nepal, including his pioneering 1950 trek into the Khumbu region. Tilman's witty, incisive writing is vastly underappreciated by those outside the mountaineering community.

■ *THAT UNTRAVELED WORLD*, Eric Shipton An autobiography that contains a chapter about his 1951 expedition to Khumbu with Edmund Hillary.

■ *SHERPAS: REFLECTIONS ON CHANGE IN HIMALAYAN NEPAL*, James Fisher (1990. $60.00. University of California Press.) A controversial look at the effects of Western influence that prompted a book-burning ceremony in Namche Bazaar.

Lobuje (16,207 feet), second-to-the-last village before Everest Base Camp.

■ *EVEREST*, Walt Unsworth (1999. $45.00. Mountaineers.) A detailed mountaineering history.

■ *TREKKING IN THE EVEREST REGION*, Jamie McGuinness (1998. $14.95. Trailblazer Publications.)

■ *TREKKING IN NEPAL: A TRAVELER'S GUIDE*, Steven Bezruchka (1997. $16.95. Mountaineers.) The seventh edition of a long-time favorite Nepal trekking guide

■ *TREKKING IN THE NEPAL HIMALAYA*, Stan Armington (1997. $17.95. Lonely Planet.) This guide has a detailed description of the standard Everest Base Camp route, and the route to Gokyo.

Kilimanjaro

Standing atop Africa's highest mountain has changed people's lives

Trekkers watching the sunrise from the 19,340-foot summit of Kilimanjaro have been known to cry, hug their climbing companions indiscriminately, and blubber on about this being the greatest moment of their lives. And why not? The five-day, 13,000-foot climb through jungle, scrubland, high-altitude desert, and vertiginous scree is a stern test of mental toughness. And they've just aced the test.

The final exam begins at 1 A.M. on summit day, when you crawl from your tent after a sleepless few hours gasping the thin air at 15,000 feet. Though the switchback trail up the summit cone is smooth and nontechnical, it is relentlessly steep, and the soft sand and scree suck at your boots. No special techniques, just put one foot in front of the other, again and again, in the face of inexorably escalating difficulty. With every yard of altitude achieved, oxygen wanes, muscles grow weary, IQ points drop away one by one. Trekkers

Campsite on the Machame route, Kilimanjaro. This trail begins on the south flank of the mountain at the village of Machame, far from the standard Marangu route used by the majority of trekkers.

who fall short of the top are typically turned back not by storm or ice or precipice, but by a simple failure of will: At some point, they decide that the summit is not worth the effort of taking one more step. Kilimanjaro calibrates mental toughness with excruciating precision, and I was about to let it take my measure.

We began in the village of Machame, at 6,000 feet on the south flank of the mountain, far from the standard Marangu route used by the vast majority of Kili aspirants. The Machame route is much less crowded, more scenic, and longer—five days up instead of four—which allows more time for acclimatizing to the altitude. Our group of seven climbers (five men and two women), supported by a dozen porters and guides, ranged in age from 25 to 62, in temperament from ditzy to laconic, in fitness from decent to superb. Our professions included astronomer, social worker, agronomist, hardware store manager, and titan of industry.

As we ascended the gradual lower slopes, the mossy humid jungle gave way to a forest of giant heather and pine trees. On day two, we camped at 12,600 feet on the rocky Shira Plateau

and gazed up through broken clouds at the summit, more than a mile above. It seemed inconceivable that we could actually make it up there. The next day we made a long traverse along the southern flank of the mountain to the edge of a monstrous abyss with the redundant name of Barranco Canyon. That night, the sky cleared and I was awakened at 3 A.M. by a brilliant full moon. Sticking my head from the tent flap, I was startled by the moonlit snow-clad summit, now looming larger than ever. Inconceivable.

The next day we pushed on through fog and drizzle to our final jumping-off spot for the summit attempt: Barafu Hut, a grungy, graffiti-covered tin hut on a pile of rocks at 15,000 feet, just below the mountain's steep summit cone. I was too nervous to sleep that night, and lay staring at the ceiling, waiting for the midnight wake-up call. To make matters worse, my stomach was feeling queasy. (Altitude? Disagreeable food? Nerves?)

We set off under a full moon, the snows of Kilimanjaro glowing above and the lights of Africa twinkling below. The ascent was very steep, the footing poor in loose sand and scree. Single file, our headlamps turned off in the bright moonlight,

AT A GLANCE

TRIP LENGTH 10–20 days	**PRICE RANGE (INDEPENDENT TREK)** $500–$700
TIME ON TREK 5–8 days (depends on route)	**PRICE RANGE (OUTFITTED GROUP TREK)** $700–$4,000
WALKING DISTANCE 25–35 miles	
MAXIMUM ALTITUDE 19,340 feet	**PRIME TIME** January–February, June–October
PHYSICAL CHALLENGE 1 2 3 4 ⑤	**STAGING CITY** Arusha, Tanzania, or Nairobi, Kenya
MENTAL CHALLENGE 1 2 3 4 ⑤	

Elephants beneath Kilimanjaro. This view of Africa's tallest mountain is from Amboseli Park, Kenya.

we plodded rhythmically upward. Lift a foot, move it forward eight or ten inches, put it down. Take a deep breath and do it again. Step, breathe. Step, breathe. Our Tanzanian guides chanted a soft Swahili song to keep us in a rhythm. Step, breathe, step, breathe. "Poli, poli," the guides kept saying. Slow. Slow.

My stomach got worse. Jay the astronomer offered some Pepto-Bismol pills that helped a little. Step, breathe. Step, breathe. But the nausea wouldn't go away. Step. Breathe. Puke. Only five or six more hours of this. Keep going. Concentrate. Step. Breathe. Puke.

So it went, stepping and breathing and puking in the moonlight. The lack of oxygen sucked the mental energy right out of me. The world shrank; all that existed were the dusty footprints and the boot heels of the trekker in front of me. By 17,000 feet I stopped taking the stomach pills because the task of unwrapping them was simply too difficult. At 18,000 feet, I debated long and hard whether it was worth the effort to occasionally raise my head and look at the extraordinary moonlit mountain scenery around me. Naaaah.

Then—ten minutes later? An hour?—I heard a shout from above. "Nineteen thousand! We're almost there!" Suddenly, magically, we were standing on the crater rim at Stella Point. We cheered. We hugged each other. Don the agronomy professor broke down and cried. And then the dawn began.

We rested for a while, watching mesmerized as the eastern sky turned red, casting the glaciers behind us in an eerie glow. Feeling an extraordinary exhilaration. I turned to Don and said, "Am I crazy, or is this the greatest moment of your life, too?" He pondered a moment before replying, "Well, I guess watching my son graduate from West Point might have been a little better."

We strolled over thin crunchy snow to a gentle bulge on the far side of the rim called Uhuru Peak, the highest point on the mountain. Nausea gone, I still felt light-headed and brain-dead; the task of removing my point-and-shoot

ALTITUDE SICKNESS

Altitude is the 800-pound gorilla of any Kilimanjaro trek. The thin air and lack of oxygen above 12,000 feet or so affect a trekker's every move by robbing him of strength, stamina, sleep, appetite, and IQ points. At its worst, altitude can disable and kill. How well a Kili trekker copes with the altitude is the single greatest factor in the success or failure of the climb.

Beyond mere huffing and puffing, some people begin to suffer symptoms such as headache, nausea, and lethargy as low as 8,000 feet. Above 12,000 feet or so, virtually everybody suffers a bit, at least initially. As altitude increases, symptoms can become more severe, including potentially fatal cerebral and pulmonary edema. Oddly, altitude sickness seems to strike almost at random; a vegetarian marathon runner may be laid low while the fat, chain-smoking slob in the next tent does just fine. One theory says that one's susceptibility to altitude sickness depends on one's involuntary background breathing rate, or hypoxic ventilatory response (the higher, the better). And no, there's nothing you can do to improve yours. It's a built-in genetic trait.

Fortunately, there's a lot you can do to combat altitude sickness. The most important thing is to ascend gradually once you get above 10,000 feet or so—ideally, no more than 1,000 feet per day. This gives the body time to acclimatize by building up extra red blood cells and growing more capillaries. For this reason, the longer routes like the Machame and Shira Plateau routes are the safest, and have the highest likelihood of success. The standard five-day Marangu climb is notorious for its high rate of altitude sickness and low proportion of climbers reaching the summit—only about 10 percent. Barely half even make it to the crater rim at Gillman's Point.

You also need to guzzle water until your stomach and bladder are ready to burst. (If your urine is yellow, drink more; it should be as clear as vodka.) This helps to keep your blood at the proper level of acidity, which affects your natural breathing rate. Finally, take Diamox, a prescription diuretic that has been shown to prevent or delay altitude sickness in most people.

Sunrise over Mawenzi Peak seen from Uhuru Peak, Kilimanjaro's 19,340-foot summit.

Top: Kersten Glacier at sunrise, seen from the summit of Kilimanjaro. Above: Three Masai boys near the Monduli Mountains, 50 miles west of Kilimanjaro.

camera from my pocket, aiming it, and pressing the shutter button for the obligatory summit shot used up every single IQ point I possessed. As we stood there, the sun burst out from below the horizon, and we turned to see the mountain's shadow behind us, a crisp black triangle stretching to the horizon.

We went down the Marangu Route. With long, leaping glissades in the soft sand we descended the summit cone, so arduously gained, in a couple of hours. The oxygen-rich air at 15,000 feet was wine in my lungs. We passed perhaps a hundred trekkers advancing up the lower slopes, the first people we'd seen in five days.

"Did you make the top?" they asked eagerly.

"How was it?"

"Not bad," we answered.

THE ROUTE

There are a number of routes up Kilimanjaro. The Marangu, the standard five-day tourist route, is crowded and doesn't offer much time for altitude acclimatization. Much preferable are the seven-day Machame Route, described in the narrative, and the eight-day Shira Plateau route.

WHAT TO EXPECT

Only once in my life have I been as physically and mentally wasted as I was after climbing Kili; that was after running the New York Marathon. The first few days of the trek are easy enough, with moderate ascents averaging 2,000 to 3,000 feet per day at relatively low altitude. But summit day is an 18-hour physical and mental ordeal that will test your mettle like no other trek in these pages.

Weather is typically benign by mountain standards. Although it's cold on top (typically around 30°F, but somehow it felt much colder), the likelihood of a storm is small. It's usually clear on top early in the morning. The trail is smooth and well marked, with a bit of scrambling required along the Machame Route in Barranco Canyon. There are usually a few inches of snow on the crater rim, but crampons aren't necessary.

Don't expect interesting Nepal-like villages along the way. Because Kilimanjaro is an anomaly in the African landscape—a single mountain jutting out of a vast plain—a high-altitude culture never evolved. Virtually no one lives above the handful of villages at around 6,000 feet.

GUIDES AND OUTFITTERS

Kilimanjaro offers a number of choices, none of them dirt cheap due to the high park and hut fees, which total $300 to $400 depending on the route. Do-it-yourselfers are out of luck; guides and at least one porter are required on the mountain. The least expensive option is simply

Sunset, summit of Mount Kilimanjaro along the Machame route.

to show up in the town of Marangu, at the foot of the mountain, and hire a guide and porters on the spot. If you supply your own food and equipment and do your own cooking, the standard five-day Marangu Route can cost as little as $500, including the park fees. The Machame Route can be done this way for as little as $700. At this bottom-of-the-barrel price, expect bottom-of-the-barrel competence and reliability from your guide. (Some Kili guides have been known to dawdle along so that they will conveniently run out of time and not have to escort their clients all the way to the top. And many guides on the quickie Marangu route take climbers only to Gillman's Point on the crater rim, not the actual summit at Uhuru Peak.)

LOCAL OUTFITTERS

A better choice is a full-service trek organized by any number of outfitters in the towns of Arusha, Moshe, or Marangu. They typically charge $700 to $800 for the quickie five-day Marangu climb. The Machame and Shira Plateau routes cost more due to the longer time spent in the park (fees are on a per-day basis) and the more complex logistics. A seven-

Descent from Kili. The volcanic peak is one of the world's tallest freestanding mountains.

day Machame climb, booked in Marangu, at the base of the mountain, typically costs $1,000 to $1,200, again with no hotels. A recommended outfitter is the Marangu Hotel (011-255-55-50639, marangu@users.africaonline.co.ke)

U.S. OUTFITTERS

Kilimanjaro climb packages booked in Arusha, Tanzania's main city, typically include transportation to and from the mountain and hotel stays before and after the climb. Figure $1,200 for the Marangu route, and $1,500 for the Machame. American agents such as Africa Adventure Company (800-882-9453, africa-adventure.com) and Thomson Safaris (see list) can book these Arusha-based trips.

Kilimanjaro climb packages from American outfitters are much more expensive. But they typically include a game-viewing mini-safari before or after the climb, transportation from the airport, first-class hotels and meals before and after the climb, a Western trip leader, and various logistical backup and safety measures. And, no small matter, they really want to get you to the summit. Figure $3,000 to $3,500 for the Machame route. Among the many U.S. outfitters offering Kilimanjaro/safari packages are:

ALPINE ASCENTS INTERNATIONAL
206-378-1927
www.alpineascents.com
GEOGRAPHIC EXPEDITIONS
800-777-8183
www.geoex.com
MOUNTAIN TRAVEL-SOBEK
800-227-2384
www.mtsobek.com
SUMMITS ADVENTURE TRAVEL
360-569-2993
summitsadventure.com
THOMSON SAFARIS
800-235-0829
www.thomsonsafaris.com
WILDERNESS TRAVEL
800-368-2794
www.wildernesstravel.com

RECOMMENDED READING
■ *THE SNOWS OF KILIMANJARO*, Ernest Hemingway ($9.00. Simon & Schuster.) Harry found his heaven in the great mountain. Maybe you will, too.
■ *THE SHADOW OF KILIMANJARO: ON FOOT ACROSS EAST AFRICA*, Rick Ridgeway (2000.

Box at Kili's summit containing a logbook in which trekkers may record their triumph.

$14.95. Henry Holt.) The author walks from the summit of Kilimanjaro to the Indian Ocean.
■ *KILIMANJARO & MOUNT KENYA: A CLIMBING AND TREKKING GUIDE*, Cameron M. Burns (1998. $18.95. Mountaineers.) A detailed trekking guide, with information about little-known back routes.
■ *TREKKING IN EAST AFRICA*, David Else (1998. $17.95. Lonely Planet.) A Lonely Planet guide with a long Kilimanjaro section.

Snow Lake

"... beyond all comparison the finest view of mountains it has ever been my lot to behold..."

Which is the most beautiful mountain vista in the world?

Veteran trekkers are typically reluctant to answer this question flat out. They'll hem and haw and say something like, well, it's all a matter of taste. To debate the aesthetic merits of Grand Teton, Ama Dablam, and Fitzroy is as fruitless as trying to rank those of, say, Marilyn Monroe, Catherine Deneuve, and Halle Berry.

But there's one place, in remote northeastern Pakistan, that is so overpowering in its visual eloquence and drama that a number of qualified observers have been willing to put aside the dithering and declare unequivocally that this is The Place. The Most Beautiful Place in the World.

The Place is improbably remote, a week's trek from the nearest human habitation, which is itself the last outpost in the hardscrabble frontier region of Baltistan. Perhaps the difficulty of trekking to The Place—only about 200 people a year

Balti horse caravan, Suru Valley, Ladakh region of India south of the line of control claimed by Pakistan.

manage to reach it—and the lack of oxygen at its rather extreme altitude have colored the aesthetic judgment of those who have been there. Perhaps not.

The Place is called Lupke Lawo, or Snow Lake. It's not a lake, but a ten-mile-wide basin of ice at 16,000 feet ringed by the jagged high peaks of the Karakoram Range. Punctuated by mountainous "islands" that jut from its surface, Snow Lake lies at the head of the Biafo and Hispar glaciers, which spread down from it like a long, bony thumb and little finger, together forming an 81-mile river of ice that is among the world's longest continuous glacier systems outside of the polar regions.

The first Westerner—and perhaps the first human—to see The Place was the British explorer Sir Martin Conway, who journeyed there in 1892. A veteran mountaineer, he had spent most of his life exploring the Alps and Himalayas, and it is unlikely that anyone then alive had seen more of the world's mountain scenery than he had. Here is how Conway described his first sight of Snow Lake as his party crested the pass at the top of the Hispar Glacier:

"We expected to look down a long valley such as we had come up, but there was no valley in sight. Before us lay a basin or lake of snow. It was beyond all comparison the finest view of mountains it has ever been my lot to behold, nor do I believe the world can hold a finer. . . . I forgot headache, food, everything, in the overwhelming impression this majestic scene left upon me, and the hour and a quarter we were privileged to gaze upon it passed like the dream of a moment."

He named the place Snow Lake.

Modern visitors are no less exuberant in their aesthetic judgments. "I totally agree with Conway," says Cameron Wake, a glaciologist who has visited Snow Lake four times and once spent two months camped out there. "Pick out any grandiose adjective you want, and it applies. I've been to a lot of mountains, but Snow Lake is definitely the most spectacular place I've ever seen."

AT A GLANCE

TRIP LENGTH 21–28 days	**PRICE RANGE (INDEPENDENT TREK)** $1,300–$1,500
TIME ON TREK 12–16 days	
WALKING DISTANCE 120 miles	**PRICE RANGE (OUTFITTED GROUP TREK)** $1,700–$4,000
MAXIMUM ALTITUDE 16,900 feet	
PHYSICAL CHALLENGE 1 2 3 ④ 5	**PRIME TIME** July–August
MENTAL CHALLENGE 1 2 3 4 ⑤	**STAGING CITY** Islamabad, Pakistan
	HEADS UP Recurring border clashes between India and Pakistan

Moonrise over Snow Lake. Alpenglow is illuminating Baintha Brakk *(the Ogre), the rock spire on the right.*

Conway's trek up the Hispar Glacier to 16,900-foot Hispar La pass, across the edge of Snow Lake, then down the Biafo Glacier to the village of Askole was the first documented human traverse between the neighboring kingdoms of Hunza and Baltistan, which historically had no contact with each other due to the formidable intervening terrain. Local legend, however, tells of a band of 800 men from Hunza who once trekked the route in the 19th century to loot Balti villages, supposedly making off not only with cows, sheep, and goats, but a number of Balti women as well. (The legend gave no details about how the raiders managed to actually transport and feed the cows, sheep, and, goats—not to mention the women—during the arduous two-week return trip.)

Interestingly enough, Conway did not share the Hunza men's fascination with the charms of Balti women. Quite the contrary, in fact. Proving once again that he was not faint-hearted when it came to aesthetic calibration, he described the women of Askole as "a most ill-looking lot." Indeed, when Conway and his men sang their favorite bawdy song around the campfire, a ditty that went:

We love you all
Petite and tall
Whate'er your beauty or grade is...
Coy or coquette
Blondes or brunettes
We love you all, bewitching ladies

Porters carry supplies and equipment to the moraine that runs up the center of Biafo Glacier.

Conway cautioned that "a mental reservation had certainly to be made for the hags of Askole."

Perhaps there's only so much beauty to go around in the Karakoram, and the mountains got all of it. Or perhaps Conway's capacity for aesthetic appreciation had been blunted by the constant onslaught of voluptuous visuals from the landscape itself. No matter. If you want pretty women with your mountains, go to Aspen.

THE ROUTE

Modern-day trekkers follow in Conway's footsteps almost exactly—but in the reverse direction. Also known as the Biafo-Hispar Glacial Traverse, the journey to Snow Lake typically begins in Islamabad, the main jumping-off spot for mountaineers and trekkers into the Karakoram Range. After driving or flying (weather permitting) from Islamabad to Skardu, trekkers travel by jeep along the terrifyingly narrow and precipitous road through the Braldu Gorge to the remote village of Askole, where the trek begins. (It's sometimes necessary to walk the last few miles to Askole due to washed-out roads.) The trek route proceeds briefly up the Baltoro Glacier towards K2, then turns northwest up the Biafo Glacier for about a week to Snow Lake. From there, trekkers cross the pass at Hispar La and make the five- to six-day descent of the Hispar Glacier to the Hunza Valley, the lush green oasis that was supposedly the inspiration for James Hilton's Shangri-La. Return is via jeep to Karimabad and Gilgit, then by plane or jeep (depending on weather) to Islamabad.

WHAT TO EXPECT

Askole, the starting point for the trek, is a grim, charmless, medieval village of about 500

Dachigan campground 15 miles west of Hispar Pass, Bal Chhish Range in background.

people—mostly farmers and herders—who live in mud and rock huts. There are no accommodations save for a trekkers' campground. Once out on the trail, the Snow Lake trek is in some ways easier than the typical Himalayan trek, in some ways more difficult. The ascent along a literal river of ice is a very gradual 1,000 feet per day, with no steep ups or downs. On the other hand, the footing is often tricky as you pick your way along the rubble-strewn glacier, hopping from one rock to another over sometimes slippery ice. Agility and surefootedness are nearly as important as stamina.

Unlike many other Himalayan treks, Snow Lake is entirely devoid of villages or human settlements along the route. Nepal veterans will miss the smiling kids, terraced greenery, and religious shrines, "You're completely isolated from people,"

MILE-DEEP GLACIER

In 1986, University of New Hampshire glaciologist Cameron Wake, using a radio echo-sounding device, measured the thickness of the Biafo Glacier where it flows out of Snow Lake at 1,400 meters—almost a mile. This is the thickest glacial ice ever measured outside of Antarctica and Greenland. Wake also discovered several so-called "surging glaciers" nearby, one of which moved several kilometers in the space of one year, necessitating a six-hour detour along the usual trekking route.

Wake's instruments, along the lower 20 miles of Biafo.

says Geographic Expeditions guide Vassi Koutsatiz. "There's nothing but rock and ice. It's not a pleasant environment." (Even Conway admitted that the Biafo and Hispar scenery "attracts by its grandeur but repels by its desolation.") But for those seeking solitude, remoteness, and sheer overpowering visual grandeur, this trek is unsurpassed.

Maximum altitude is an energy-sapping 16,900 feet, and you'll spend a week or so above 13,000. The gradual ascent, however, allows good acclimatization.

The Snow Lake trek is not without danger. People have died falling into crevasses on the Biafo and Hispar Glaciers. It may be necessary for trekkers to "rope up" occasionally—link themselves together with a stout climbing rope so that if one slips into a crevasse, the others can pull him out.

Weather is unpredictable along the route, with blizzards and whiteouts possible at any time.

Heavy snow can be a problem because it covers up the crevasses in the glaciers. Occasionally, groups have been forced to turn back by storms.

Constant border squabbling between Pakistan and India has scared off a number of Karakoram trekkers in recent years. Although Indian and Pakistani mountain troops have been taking potshots at each other for decades along

High-altitude porters (Husain and Mohammed) from Askole take a break beside the Braldu River.

Top: Dilapidated footbridge across the Hispar River just below Hispar village; it has been replaced. Above: Crevasse field on Hispar Pass (16,900 feet) and south wall of Hispar Pass.

1998 when American adventurer Ned Gillette was murdered in his tent by two young bandits in the Haramosh Valley, some 50 miles west of Snow Lake. But the killing appears to have been an aberration; the local inhabitants, who typically have no quarrel with foreign trekkers, were shocked by the attack.

GUIDES AND OUTFITTERS

Because Snow Lake is a week's walk from the nearest human habitation, it's simply not feasible to trek there on your own. In Skardu, the last outpost where food and fuel can be reliably obtained, you may be able to find a freelance guide who can arrange for porters, supplies, and jeeps to and from the trailheads. Typically, you'll need three or four porters per trekker, at a cost of about $100 each. Total cost of a bare-bones Snow Lake trek arranged in Skardu could be as low as $1,300 per person, depending on group size. But the competence and reliability of Skardu guides is variable; a better choice is one of several outfitters in Islamabad that offer Snow Lake trek packages at prices ranging from about $1,700 to $2,000 per person for a group of eight.

LOCAL OUTFITTERS

WALGI'S ADVENTURE PAKISTAN
011-92-51-214345
www.south-asia.com/pakistan/walji1.htm
U.S. NAZIR SABIR EXPEDITIONS
011-92-51-252553
www.nazirsabir.com

U.S. OUTFITTERS

Several U.S. outfitters offer full-service trek packages with all the amenities—hotels and meals in Islamabad, Western guides, and flights to and from Skardu and Gilgit, at prices ranging from $3,000 to $4,000. Concordia Expeditions is run by Pakistani native Masood Ahmad and his American wife Patrice. KE Adventure Travel,

the Siachen Glacier, about 75 miles from Askole, the conflict has not spilled over into the main Karakoram trekking routes. Nor has the ongoing violence in Kashmir, 150 miles to the south and across the Indian border. The Karakoram area got a jolt of bad publicity in

Sunset and moonrise, looking east up Hispar Glacier at the Bal Chhish Range two-thirds of the way down from Hispar Pass.

the American booking agent for a British company of the same name, offers two itineraries.

CONCORDIA EXPEDITIONS
719–395–9191
www.concordiaexpeditions.com
Price $3,390 for 25 days

GEOGRAPHIC EXPEDITIONS
800-888-7173
www.geoex.com
$3,995 for 27 days

KE ADVENTURE TRAVEL
800-497-9675
www.keadventure.com
$2,995 for 21 days; $3,195 for 28 days

RECOMMENDED READING

■ *TREKKING IN PAKISTAN AND INDIA*, Hugh Swift Now out of print, but a guidebook worth looking for, written by a legendary Himalayan walker.

■ *TREKKING IN THE KARAKORAM AND HINDU KUSH*, John Mock and Kimberly O'Neill (1996. $16.95. Lonely Planet.) The state-of-the-art guidebook for Snow Lake trekkers.

■ *WHERE MEN AND MOUNTAINS MEET and THE GILGIT GAME*, John Keay Adventure-book guru Tom Cole calls these books "the finest history of exploration, diplomatic wrangling, high-altitude spying, and general good fun in the western Himalayas and Karakoram."

■ *BLANK ON THE MAP*, Eric Shipton Tales of Karakoram expeditioning by the legendary British mountaineer and writer.

■ *THE KARAKORAM: MOUNTAINS OF PAKISTAN*, Shiro Shirahata (1990. $75.00. Cloudcap.) A superb coffee-table photo book.

The Paine Circuit

Surreal mountain sculpture, calving glaciers, swarms of condors, and wind—always the wind.

Not long ago, I was assigned to write an entertaining little piece for an on-line adventure travel service. The idea was to ask the founders or presidents of five leading adventure-travel companies to name the five places in the world that had stirred their hearts and souls more than any others. Not surprisingly, there was a broad spectrum of replies from this elite cadre of lifelong world travelers: the Karakoram, Tuscany, the Futaleufu River, Bali, the Galapagos.

But among these connoisseurs' picks, one stood out, the only place chosen by more than one respondent—by three of them, in fact. That place was Torres del Paine, the jagged massif of mountains that juts 6,000 feet out of the Patagonian pampas in southern Chile.

I'll not attempt to describe with words the spires, lakes, and glaciers that so stirred these veteran adventurers. (Sample gushings: "More spectacular scenery in one small area than any-

Gate to an estancia *(ranch) outpost on Lago Sarmiento and the Torres (towers) del Paine, background.*

where in the world. . . .The most dramatic mountain area on the planet. It takes my breath away every time I see it again. . . .The raw beauty keeps me going back.") The photos accompanying this text will have to do.

But there is one aspect of Paine's aesthetic drama that photos don't express well: its compact size. All the highest peaks lie within an area about ten miles square, and, standing a few miles away, one can take them all in with a single glance. The compact size of the Paine massif also inspired some adventurous soul to first say, "Hey, let's walk all the way around it." The 60-mile Paine circuit has become one of the world's great treks—and judging from the votes of the aforementioned adventure-travel connoisseurs, perhaps the finest of them all in terms of sheer overpowering visual impact.

After they have finished raving about the beauty of the place, most trekkers turn immediately to Paine Conversation Point No. 2: the wind. According to the World Survey of Climatology, during the summer months (peak trekking season) in inland Patagonia, the average reported wind speed from nine reporting points—day, night, week after week—is just under 8 meters per second, about 18 mph. The Survey authors note, however, that the "the published values of wind speed in Patagonia are certainly not representative," due to the location of most reporting stations in towns and villages, which naturally tend to be in the most sheltered places. Newer stations in less sheltered areas, they report, register average wind speeds in some cases more than 100 percent higher than the published numbers—in the range of 40 mph. A 1994 study revealed average wind speeds of up to 56 mph at one reporting point.

The Patagonian wind has been reported upon by virtually every traveler to the bottom of South America. *Grand tempeste* were mentioned in the first written dispatch from Patagonia, the journal of Antonio Pigafetta, the adventurous young Italian who on a lark joined Ferdinand Magellan's three-year round-the-world expedition in 1519. Charles Darwin wrote of the "constant succession of gales" that assaulted the H.M.S. *Beagle* during his 1834 Patagonia expedition.

AT A GLANCE

TRIP LENGTH 12–17 days
TIME ON TREK 6–10 days
WALKING DISTANCE 60 miles, plus two side hikes totaling about 35 miles
MAXIMUM ALTITUDE 3,900 feet
PHYSICAL CHALLENGE 1 2 ③ 4 5
MENTAL CHALLENGE 1 2 ③ 4 5

PRICE RANGE (INDEPENDENT TREK) $200–$350
PRICE RANGE (OUTFITTED GROUP TREK) $1,500–$4,200
PRIME TIME December–March
STAGING CITY Punta Arenas, Chile

Cuernos del Paine above grasses blowing in the relentless wind, Torres del Paine National Park.

George Gaylord Simpson, a young naturalist on a 1932 expedition to Patagonia for the American Museum of Natural History, wrote in his journal, "Justino awoke me this morning by shouting that the wind was blowing, which is like telling a sailor that the sea happens to be salty this morning. . .the fact that the air is in rapid motion becomes almost as elemental as the fact that there is air. It is a condition of life here. . . ".

On another occasion, Simpson noted, "The strongest wind I have ever seen was blowing on the barranca today. To climb over the crest, I had to crawl on my belly, and in a less cautious moment was knocked down and almost blown over a cliff. Going into the wind down a slope that was too steep to stand on at all ordinarily, we could walk leaning forward at an apparently fatal angle, supported by the constant gale in our faces . . .just there the wind was blowing such large

pebbles that we had to remove our goggles for fear of their being hit and broken."

Lady Florence Dixie, an adventurous and wealthy Victorian woman who toured Patagonia in 1880, reported that after some weeks, "a most disagreeable metamorphosis had taken place in our faces. They were swollen to an almost unrecognizable extent, had assumed a deep purple hue, the phenomenon being accompanied by sharp itching. The boisterous wind, which is the standard drawback to the otherwise agreeable climate of Patagonia, was no doubt the cause of this annoyance. . .after a few days the skin of our faces peeled off completely, but the swelling did not go down for some time. I would advise any person who makes the same journey to provide themselves with masks. . .(to) save themselves a great deal of the discomfort we suffered from the winds."

When the wind does stop, as it does every once in a while, the effect can be strange indeed. Faced with a period of absolute calm, the Patagonian explorer Eric Shipton noted, "As with the sudden cessation of an artillery barrage, the silence was uncanny, almost oppressive. It took some time to become accustomed to the strange tranquillity, and even when I awoke the next morning, I had a sense of unreality, as if a fundamental part of life was missing."

THE ROUTE

Trekkers typically fly first to Punta Arenas, then drive to Puerto Natales and on to Torres del Paine National Park.

The circuit trek typically starts near the main entrance to the park at Guarderia Laguna Amarga. With the main peaks on your left, the trail proceeds north along the Rio (River) Paine to Lago (Lake) Paine (An optional route for this first leg—less traveled and with better views of the Paine massif— skirts Lago Azul, farther to the east.) From the campsite at Lago Paine, the trail heads west along the back side of the massif to Lago Dixon. From there you'll start climbing

Balancing against wind, rock, and water, Salto Grande *(great waterfall) between Lago Nordenskjold and Lago Pehoe.*

toward glacier-fed Lago de Los Perros and up over the windy John Garner pass, the high point of the trek. (Those on outfitted trips using pack-horses will leave the horses at Lago Dixon and put on backpacks for three days.) You'll then descend very steeply on a rugged slippery trail toward the huge Grey Glacier. The route then turns back south, paralleling the Grey Glacier and Lago Grey to Rifugio Grey, a trekkers' hut with food and hot showers where group trekkers will meet their packhorses again. From there the usual route con-tinues south along Lago Grey and follows the Rio Grey back to the road and the Park Administra-tion Center, some 20 road miles south of the main entrance where the trek started.

Independent trekkers may wish to complete the circle by returning to Guarderia Laguna Amarga via a new trail along the north shore of Lago Nordenskjold. (Prepare to wade on occa-sion; footbridges across the numerous streams that pour down into the lake may be washed out.) Winds are particularly strong here. No camping is permitted along this seven-hour stretch.

Two wonderful side hikes along the route should be considered mandatory. The first, at the beginning of the trek, leads up the Ascensio Valley into the heart of the Paine Range. From a lookout point, you'll see the classic Torres del Paine travel brochure shot: the four main towers looming over a small glacial lake. The second side hike, near the

Torres del Paine from Lago Pehoe.

end of the circuit, leads up the Frances Valley. From here you'll see the Cuernos del Paine—the Horns of Paine, a pair of weirdly sculpted peaks that are also brochure favorites.

An increasingly popular alternative to the traditional full circuit is the shorter "W" route (so called because the trail routing approximates the letter's shape), which includes three out-and-back legs up the Ascensio Valley, Frances Valley, and Lago Grey to the Grey Glacier. The W is shorter, hits the main scenic high spots, and allows trekkers to stay in comfortable *rifugios* or *hosterias* each night. It lacks the ruggedness, remoteness, and sense of accomplishment of the full circuit, however.

WHAT TO EXPECT

This is a challenging trek with stretches of difficult footing and the potential for bad weather. (The wind, of course, is omnipresent.) The neces-

sity of carrying a 30 to 35-pound backpack for three days makes this walk a particular challenge (and stretches our definition of trekking a bit). One Paine trekker describes the backpacking leg down from John Garner Pass toward the Grey Glacier this way: "A real bitch: slipping, sliding, going hand-to-hand from tree to tree through a section that I traversed mostly by sitting and sliding down on my butt."

Accommodations along the way are a mixture of designated campsites (some with toilets, showers, and basic supplies, but BYO tent) and well-stocked *rifugios* with bunks, hot showers, and meals.

Don't expect to be alone in a pristine wilderness. As one of the world's great trekking and hiking areas, the Paine Circuit draws lots of people, most of them day-hikers who stick to the Ascensio Valley, Frances Valley, and the more accessible south end of the park. The huts and

Opposite: Galen Rowell, self-portrait with wind-tortured tree.

Trekker at Lago Grey. Huge chunks of Grey Glacier calve into Lago Grey, forming freshwater icebergs. The Paine Circuit follows the edge of both the glacier and the lake.

campgrounds will be crowded, and you'll have plenty of company along the trail, except on the remote northern half of the loop.

The weather is very changeable, with rain likely and snow possible at higher elevations. Water- and windproof foul weather gear is a must. If you're trekking without an outfitter, your tent should be a stout one, able to withstand very strong winds. Mostly because of the unpredictable weather, the National Park authorities do not permit solo trekking. If you're on your own, you'll have to find a trekmate on the spot.

GUIDES AND OUTFITTERS

Independent trekkers won't need a guide. The trails for the most part are well trodden and clearly marked. A good up-to-date map is a must, however. (The best one, published by

Zagier and Urruty in Argentina, is available from AdventurousTraveler.com.) Food is available at several points along the way. For *rifugio* reservations or information, call Andescape (011-56-61-412-592). Cost for a bunk is about $15 per night, or $35 with three meals.

LOCAL OUTFITTERS

A number of local outfitters in Puerto Natales offer treks in Paine. Try:

AMERINDIA EXPEDICIONES
011-56-61-410-678
amerindi@entelchile.net

U.S. OUTFITTERS

We're aware of only two American outfitters, Mountain Travel-Sobek and Southwind Adven-

tures, that still operate the full Paine Circuit trek. (The others seem to have gone "soft," offering only day hikes out of permanent lodges. Breathtakingly spectacular mountain walking, yes, but it ain't no trek.) A third company, Latin American Escapes, is the U.S. agent for a Chilean outfitter that runs the Paine Circuit trek, Santiago-based Cascada Expeditions.

MOUNTAIN TRAVEL-SOBEK
  800-227-2384
  www.mtsobek.com
  $3,800–$4,200 for 17 days
SOUTHWIND ADVENTURES
  800-377-9463
  www.southwindadventures.com
  $3,100–3,300 for 16 days
LATIN AMERICAN ESCAPES
  800-510-935-5241
  $1,540 for 14 days

RECOMMENDED READING

■ *TREKKING IN THE PATAGONIAN ANDES,* Clem Lindenmayer (1998. $17.95. Lonely Planet.) A Lonely Planet guide with a section on the Paine Circuit.

Dock with a view, Hotel Explora on Lago Pehoe.

■ *CHILE AND ARGENTINA BACKPACKING AND HIKING,* Tim Burford (1998. $17.95. Globe Pequot.) A Bradt guide with a section on Paine. Maps not as good as Lonely Planet's.
■ *DEEP PLAY,* Paul Pritchard (1998. $22.95. Mountaineers.) An award-winning memoir by a wild and crazy British big-wall climber with several chapters on his ascents of the Torres del Paine.

PAINE WILDLIFE

Confronted with the unexpected vision of what appear to be pink flamingos and ostriches along the trail, the Paine trekker may wonder if he has accidentally ingested some sort of hallucinogenic Patagonian mushroom. Nope, the birds are real. Unusual wildlife has flourished in Paine since hunting and grazing were banned in 1959, when the area became a national park. Paine was designated a United Nations Biosphere Reserve in 1978.

The birds that appear to be pink flamingoes are, well, pink flamingoes, so pink "that they seem to have been spray-painted by the Chilean tourist board," in the

words of one Paine trekker. The ostrich-looking things are rheas (known locally as nandus), three-toed flightless birds that grow up to five feet tall. In open grassy areas, you'll certainly see grazing guanacos, wild relatives of the llama and alpaca. And then there are the condors, with wingspans up to ten feet, clouds of them, perhaps more condors than anywhere else in the world. One Paine trek leader recalls, "I once had a group that saw 75 in one day. After a while, you're saying to yourself, 'Another condor. Big deal.'"

The Dolomites Traverse

Forget the Alps. Europe's most alluring mountain range has cooler-looking peaks and a double-barreled local culture: Wiener schnitzel and pizzocheri.

Walking alone among the limestone towers and pinnacles of the Dolomites, I puzzled at the absence of my countrymen from this splendid mountain tableau. In the course of a cool August morning, I had been showered with *buon giornos* and *guten Tags* from passing walkers, but not a single howya doin'. Vast hordes of Americans visit Venice, just 75 miles to the south, but apparently they all keep right on going. What are they, crazy?

The Dolomites, though adjacent to the Alps, are a different kind of mountain range altogether. They are lower in elevation—the highest Dolomite peaks top at just under 11,000 feet, nearly a mile below Mont Blanc—but most people find them more aesthetically alluring. Instead of the usual massive snowcapped movie-logo pyramids, trekkers gaze up at impetuous, delicate pinnacles and spires of bare white carbonate stone. Along Alta Via 1, the showpiece trekking

Peasant harvesting wheat on a hill farm in the fabled Fanes region of the northern Dolomites.

route that cuts through the heart of the range from north to south, peaks like Monte Pelmo and Monte Civetta, with their ramparts and towers jutting dramatically out of the smooth landscape around them, resemble huge castles. When the clouds and the light are just so, they seem to float in the air, Magritte paintings come to life.

Along Alta Via 1, as well as in the rest of the Dolomites, is a superb system of *rifugios*, the comfortable backcountry mountain "huts" (more like small rustic hotels, actually) that are a staple of European trekking but virtually unknown in the United States. (We're starting to catch on, though; the Tenth Mountain Trail hut system that links Aspen and Vail is a fair imitation.) Resupplied by helicopter, ski lift, mule, or jeep, the *rifugios* feature warm bunks, good food and drink, and unmatched international gemutlichkeit once the sun goes down.

The villages of the Dolomites look more Austrian than Italian—tidy chalet-style houses, red flowers in window boxes, Mercedes taxicabs. That's no surprise; the Dolomites and the sur-rounding region of South Tyrol were a part of the Austro-Hungarian Empire for centuries. The locals spoke German and wore lederhosen. When World War I broke out, thousands of young men from Dolomite villages were shipped off to fight on the Russian front. In 1915, Italy jumped into the war on the Allied side, and as Italian troops pushed northward, the outmanned Austrians took to the mountaintops and dug in for what turned out to be a bloody, pointless three-year standoff—a literal inversion of the futile slaughter in the trenches 600 miles north.

As part of the postwar peace treaty, the Italo-Austrian border was moved northward about 50 miles to its present position at the Brenner Pass. Overnight the Dolomites became Italian, and Rome quickly began a campaign to wipe out the old Germanic ways. Carabinieri went from house to house ripping down portraits of the Kaiser, and every town, river, and mountain was rechristened with an Italian name.

Over the intervening years, ethnic tensions have eased, if not dissolved. Tyrolean culture has

AT A GLANCE

TRIP LENGTH 11 days	PRICE RANGE (INDEPENDENT TREK) $300–$400
TIME ON TREK 9 days	PRICE RANGE (OUTFITTED GROUP TREK)
WALKING DISTANCE 49 miles	$1,500–$3,500
MAXIMUM ALTITUDE 10,000 feet	PRIME TIME Mid-June–mid-September (Avoid August,
PHYSICAL CHALLENGE 1 ② 3 4 5	European holiday month; trails and huts are crowded.)
MENTAL CHALLENGE ① 2 3 4 5	STAGING CITY Innsbruck, Austria (Also Bolzano,
	Verona, or Venice, Italy)

resurfaced, and towns and mountains now have dual names. (I stayed in a town with the typically dissonant moniker of Selva-Wolkenstein.) Today Tyroleans and Italians coexist in a cordial apartheid, with generally separate schools and social groups, but a common appreciation for their pastoral surroundings and the tourist dollar.

Oddly, Dolomites residents have chosen not to erase the physical scars of their past conflicts. Eighty-five years later, the detritus of the Great War is still strewn about the landscape. A trekker may stumble across strands of barbed wire, spent bullets, ration cans, shell casings, even shreds of leather combat boots. Crumbling battlements, tunnels, precarious steel cables and ladders, and bomb craters still dot the landscape north and west of Cortina, site of the fiercest fighting. One still-visible scar of war along Alta Via 1 is the rubble-strewn Pico Lagazuoi, where the Italians spent six months digging a tunnel a half a mile into the mountain to plant 35 tons of blasting gelatin. But the Austrians, having felt the vibrations of the tunneling machinery, had already abandoned their position on the summit. The ensuing futile explosion literally blew off the top of the mountain. (One of the remaining tunnels is open to hikers.)

Such puny efforts of man have done little to diminish the richly textured landscape that has attracted Europe's creative elite for centuries. Gustav Mahler spent summers in the Dolomite village of Toblach, where he composed *Das Lied von der Erde* and the Ninth Symphony while his wife had an affair with a young pianist who was their houseguest. Franz Kafka wrote back to his lady friend Milena, "What a country this is! Heavens. . .if you were only here. . . ." Henrik Ibsen, visiting with his wife and son, fell scandalously in love with an 18-year old girl (Henrik was 61 at the time.)The dour dramatist's Dolomite dalliance fizzled when her parents took her back home to Vienna, but he wrote her passionate letters for years.

Is there something in the thrusting pinnacles of the Dolomites that encourages romantic longing? What to make of the fact that Mahler, Kafka, and Ibsen—not the three most lighthearted, happy-go-lucky guys in the world—all were drawn to a mountain range known for its light, airy, almost playful landscapes? In these questions lurk at least two Ph.D. theses.

And speaking of lighthearted, happy-go-lucky guys, we mustn't ignore Ezra Pound, the irascible American poet whose daughter by his mistress was born in the Dolomites and raised by a local farm family. After the fall of Mussolini in 1943, Pound trekked 100 miles from Verona through the mountains to tell his daughter, by now 18 years old, that he in fact had another family. It wasn't long thereafter that Pound's pro-Fascist radio broadcasts from Rome got him arrested for treason by advancing U.S. troops. A jury declared him unfit to stand trial due to an "unsound mind," and he was committed to a psychiatric hospital in Washington D.C. for 12 years. Upon his release in 1958, Pound immediately fled

*Opposite: Trekker in a valley below Monte Civetta, one of the Dolomites' most dramatic peaks, rising to over 9,600 feet in the heart of the region. Above: A peak in the Sassolungo group (*Langkofel *in German and literally "long stone" in English).*

Rock climber on limestone outcrops on the way to climb Cinque Torres (Five Towers), a center for technical climbing.

back to northern Italy, where he lived in a castle on a hill just west of the Dolomites with his daughter and granddaughter. He did some gardening, wrote some poems, and watched the sun rise over spires and ramparts of rose-colored rock. Now, who's crazy?

THE ROUTE

This trek essentially follows Alta Via 1, a long-distance walking route that traverses the Dolomites along the north-south axis. For the north-to-south trek described here, Innsbruck, Austria is the most convenient staging city. From there, you'll drive south through the Brenner Pass to Welsberg, Italy. The trek begins at Pragser Wildsee (also known as Lago di Braies) and proceeds up to 7,900-foot Porta sora L'Fom pass, from which you can see to the south the limestone peaks of Tofane, Pelmo, Cristallo, and Civetta, which line your route for the next week or so. You'll proceed south through the Alpo de Lagazuoi and its World War I tunnels, the Cinque

Torres (Five Towers), the 4-mile-long wall of Monte Civetta, down the valley of Val Corpassa and its 2,000-foot rock faces. You'll finish at the Passo Duran. From there, you'll head back to Innsbruck—unless, of course you want to extend your stay and try some rock climbing. A century ago, the Dolomites were the cradle of technical big-wall rock climbing, and they remain one of the world's premiere climbing areas.

WHAT TO EXPECT

What *not* to expect is the feeling that you're in remote wilderness. The Dolomites have long been a popular walking (and skiing) area among Europeans, and you will see lots of hikers, huts, trail signs, and other markers of civilization. Ski lifts may be used occasionally to save time and/or energy. Many of the *rifugios* have dirt roads or jeep trails leading to them. All this civilization, however, makes it relatively easy to just show up and wing it without an outfitter, thereby injecting a bit of extra adventurous serendipity to your trip.

Although altitude is modest, trails can be steep in places, with daily altitude gains and losses of more than 3,000 feet. The mostly smooth and well-maintained paths may occasionally be loose, rubbly, or snow-covered. Although the Alta Via 1 route described above doesn't include any *via ferrata*, many Dolomite trails do include the so-called "iron paths," the ladders, steps, and cables installed

WAR AND REMEMBRANCE

One of the legendary heroes of the Dolomites is Sepp Innerkofler, a turn-of-the-century Tyrolean mountain climber. Swept up in World War I, he was ordered by an ignorant Austrian commander to lead a five-man assault team up the steep northwest face of Monte Paterno; its summit was held by Italian forces. Innerkofler, 50 years old at the time, had been the first man to scale the northwest ridge, and he knew that such an attack was utter folly. But he stoically followed orders. (He did, however, refuse his son's entreaties to accompany him, explaining, "Your mother must weep for only one of us.") Starting the climb in the dark, he soon outpaced his four companions, and as he neared the fortified summit, Innerkofler was alone in the light of dawn.

It's not clear what happened next, only that Innerkofler fell to his death. At first it was thought that an Italian soldier, waiting above in ambush, had dropped a boulder on him, knocking him off a ledge. But after the war, Innerkofler's exhumed body was found to have what appeared to be machine-gun bullet wounds. The most accepted account today is that Innerkofler was shot off the mountain by inept Austrian troops on the ground below, who mistook him for an Italian. His gravestone, a grim reminder of the tragic futility of the Dolomite campaign, is there on the summit of Monte Paterno today.

World War I Italian cannon being hoisted into place in 1916.

Overleaf: Rifugio Locatelli overlooking Monte Paterno (left) and Tre Cime (Three Peaks) di Lavaredo.

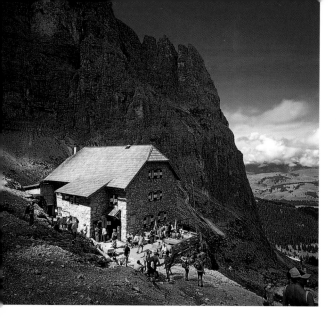

Rifugio Vicenza, in the heart of the Sassolungo group, was built in 1894 and rebuilt in 1903 after being destroyed by an avalanche.

over the years (some as far back as World War I) to help trekkers scramble over particularly steep or tricky sections that would otherwise require technical climbing gear. If you have a fear of heights, or poor agility, avoid the *via ferrata*.

The *rifugios* vary in capacity from 20 to about 40. Typically there are several bunkrooms with four to eight bunks each. Blankets and pillows are provided. (No sleeping bags needed.) Most *rifugios* have hot showers. And, if you absolutely have to check on your Microsoft stock, virtually all *rifugios* have telephones. Continental breakfast is served around 7:30 each morning, and a fixed-menu dinner is typically served around 7:00 P.M. Lights go out promptly at 10:00 P.M.

GUIDES AND OUTFITTERS

Because of the presence of the *rifugios* all along the route, this is an easy trek to do on your own, and you can take your pick of literally hundreds of other routes throughout the Dolomites. The *rifugios* should be booked a few days beforehand, however, particularly in August and on

weekends. *Rifugios* typically charge $25 to $30 a night, including dinner and continental breakfast. Figure another $10 to $15 a day for a *rifugio* lunch and a beer or two with dinner.

LOCAL OUTFITTERS

Local guides are available everywhere throughout the Dolomites. Check with village tourist offices when you arrive for a list of names of approved guides.

An Italian trekking company that offers full-service Dolomites treks is Scuola Alpina Dolomiten (011-39-471-70-53-43) in the village of Castelrotto.

U.S. OUTFITTERS

We're aware of only one U.S. outfitter that offers a full-service trek along the general route of Alta Via 1. Distant Journeys is run by Andrea Ellison and Julie Head, who also work as instructors at Hurricane Island Outward Bound School in Maine. One or the other leads every Alta Via 1 trek. The price includes *rifugios*, hotels, meals, and transportation between Innsbruck and the trek start and finish points.

DISTANT JOURNEYS

888-845-5781
www.distantjourneys.com
$1,895 for 9 days

A number of U.S. outfitters offer full-service treks and hikes in other parts of the Dolomites. Those of Above the Clouds (800-233-4499), Penny Pitou Travel (800-552-4661), and Alternative Travel (800-527-5997) are point-to-point treks involving *rifugio* stays, while Backroads (800-462-2483), Butterfield & Robinson (800-678-1147), Mountain Travel-Sobek (800-227-2384), Summits Adventure Travel (360-569-2993), Walking Softly Adventures (888-743-0723), and Wilderness Travel (800-368-2794) offer somewhat "softer" trips in which walkers stay in village hotels and make dayhikes. Some involve a night or two in a *rifugio*.

RECOMMENDED READING

■ *UNTRODDEN PEAKS AND UNFREQUENTED VALLEYS : A MIDSUMMER RAMBLE IN THE DOLOMITES*, Amelia B. Edwards A Victorian lady's excellent adventures.

■ *THE SUNNY SIDE OF THE ALPS*, Paul Hoffman (1995. $22.50. Henry Holt.) An entertaining history of the Dolomites and South Tyrol region.

■ *ALTA VIA: HIGH LEVEL WALKS IN THE DOLOMITES*, Martin Collins A small idiosyncratic British guidebook with detailed instructions for trekking Alta Via 1, as well as the parallel track to the west, Alta Via 2.

■ *WALKING IN THE DOLOMITES*, Gillian Price A guidebook with route descriptions for 32 short (1-4 days) walks throughout the Dolomites.

■ *VIA FERRATA: SCRAMBLES IN THE DOLOMITES*, Hofler & Werner A guidebook to the *via ferrata*, the "iron roads" through the Dolomites that consist of metal ladders, steps, and cables to assist scramblers through particularly steep or rough areas. Not for the faint-hearted.

CORAL PINNACLES

The Dolomites are named for the French mineralogist, Deodar de Dolomieu, who first analyzed their distinctive composition in 1788. (He eventually wrote up his findings in the margins of a Bible while in prison, but that's another story.) He found that the Dolomites are primarily calcium magnesium carbonate—remnants of ancient coral reefs from a 250-million year-old tropical sea. About 60 million years ago, Africa started moving north, and the tectonic pressure as it collided with Europe lifted and folded the seabed and its coral reefs into the fantastic spires we see today. The Alps were also lifted by that same geological cataclysm, but, due to their unfortunate status as ordinary dry land 250 million years ago, today they are merely run-of-the-mill mountains.

The Ruwenzori

Dreary weather, swampy trails, dicey local politics.
Is this trek worth it? Yes.

White men were talking on the tele-phone and measuring the speed of light before they managed to locate the highest mountain range in Africa. The Ruwenzori, rising 16,763 feet from the implacable dark heart of the continent, have for centuries been moun-tains of legend and illusion, shrouded in a histor-ical fog, and in a quite literal one as well.

Herodotus, the first great African traveler, pondered how the world's largest river could flow 2,000 miles out of a parched desert where rain never fell. He theorized that the source of the Nile must be melting snow "from parts beyond." On an exploratory journey up the Nile in 450 B.C., he was told by an Abyssinian sorcerer that the river flowed from a bottomless spring between two snowcapped peaks somewhere in central Africa. A hundred years later, Aristotle himself declared the source of the Nile was "the Silver Mountain."

Bakonjo porters heading up the Bujuku Valley, above Bigo Bog; Mount Stanley is in the distance.

In A.D. 120 the Syrian geographer Marinus of Tyre wrote of a Greek merchant seaman who had traveled inland from Zanzibar for 25 days and found a "silvery" mountain range that fed the Nile. Based on that account, Ptolemy, in A.D. 150, depicted the mountains on his celebrated map of the world. Apparently mistranslating "silvery" as "moon"—or perhaps simply displaying a flair for hype—Ptolemy called them *Lunae Montes*, or Mountains of the Moon. Thus grew the legend, spawned by a sorcerer's vision and nurtured by a catchy nickname.

For the next 1,700 years or so, every expedition that set out to find the source of the Nile returned a failure, or not at all. In 1876, while on the march through what was then called West Benga (and is today western Uganda), the journalist-explorer Henry Morton Stanley—the man who had five years earlier uttered the immortal "Dr. Livingstone, I presume"—"obtained a faint view of an enormous blue mass afar off." Offhandedly naming the distant range Mount Gordon-Bennett, after the degenerate drunken editor of the *New York Herald* (the chief underwriter of his expedition), Stanley unaccountably kept going, entirely unaware that he had seen the legendary mountains. Ironically, Stanley subsequently claimed that his expedition had "in my opinion, proved the nonexistence of those Mountains of the Moon that had been drawn across Africa since Ptolemy's time."

Twelve years later, on an expedition to rescue Emin Pasha, the beleaguered governor of the British colonial province of Equatoria, Stanley nearly botched it a second time. Two of his staff officers, scouting ahead of the main expedition, looked up through a break in the interminable cloud cover and saw, to their utter astonishment, a huge snowcapped mountain. When one of the officers, Arthur Jephson, informed Stanley of the brief sighting, "he laughed at me and pooh-poohed the idea," Jephson later recalled.

A month later, however, the clouds briefly thinned again, and this time Stanley was in the

---

AT A GLANCE

TRIP LENGTH 18–20 days	**PRICE RANGE (INDEPENDENT TREK)** $300*
TIME ON TREK 6–11 days	**PRICE RANGE (OUTFITTED GROUP TREK)**
WALKING DISTANCE 40 miles	$300–$3,000*
MAXIMUM ALTITUDE 14,300 feet	**PRIME TIME** December–January, June–August
PHYSICAL CHALLENGE 1 2 ③ 4 5	**STAGING CITY** Kampala or Kasese, Uganda
MENTAL CHALLENGE 1 2 3 ④ 5	(Kampala is the major city from which you would catch a plane or bus to Kasese.)

HEADS UP *At press time, trekking route was closed due to civil war in the Congo

right place at the right time. "While looking to the southeast. . .my eyes were directed by a boy to a mountain said to be covered with salt and I saw a peculiar shaped cloud of the most beautiful silver color. . . .I became conscious that what I gazed upon was not the image or semblance of a vast mountain, but the solid substance of a real one, with its summit covered in snow. . . .I have discovered the long lost snowy Mountains of the Moon, the source of. . .the Nile." His account conveniently failed to disclose that his staff officer Jephson had sighted the mountain a month previously and called it to Stanley's attention.

The Mountains of the Moon are now fully mapped and documented, of course. (And one of the main peaks is called Mount Stanley.) They have been confirmed as a source of the Nile, and there is a deep lake between two of its snow-capped peaks, just as the Abyssinian sorcerer had promised. But the precision of modern geography has little diminished the air of mystery that surrounds these mountains, now called the Ruwenzori (the name is an amalgam of local dialect names for the mountain range, all roughly meaning "Hill of Rain"). This is due partly to the perpetual mists and clouds that shroud the mountains nine days out of ten, which concealed them

Grinding corn, Kaabong, Karamoja region, Uganda.

from any number of unsuspecting explorers who passed nearby. A. F. R. Wollaston, a British naturalist who was among the first to study the area in 1906, wrote, "I was for many days a short distance from the mountains, and could not have even suspected their existence." When the Ruwenzori do reveal themselves, it is usually in brief ethereal glimpses through gaps in the clouds, as Stanley experienced. "I rubbed my eyes and wondered whether the snowpeak had been a reality or a dream," wrote Wollaston when he finally saw one of the massif's 20 summits after many weeks among them.

Lending a further air of mystery to the Ruwenzori is the bizarre natural topiary that adorn their slopes. The botanist Wollaston, scarcely able to believe his eyes, called the plant life "unworldly." D. W. Freshfield, an early Ruwenzori wanderer, wrote, "That enchanted forest has a weird and grotesque effect that is all its own. . . in rain, a nightmare. . .in the rare sunshine, a Russian pantomime. . . ." The Duke of Abruzzi, the Italian climber who was the first to reach the main Ruwenzori summits in 1906, wrote of the lower slopes through which today's trekking route meanders, "No forest can be grimmer or stranger than this."

An unusual combination of factors—steady moderate temperatures, copious rainfall (15 to 20 inches in some months), and intense ultraviolet radiation at this high elevation and low latitude—triggers in the Ruwenzori a botanical phenomenon called equatorial alpine gigantism. Grass grows 10 feet tall. Moss cushions are a foot thick. Heather plants grow 60 to 70 feet high, with lichen dripping from their twisted limbs. Groundsel and lobelia, familiar at home a few inches high, grow to four times the height of a man here, and their phallic upper pods are the size and shape of a heat-seeking missile. Guy Yeoman, a modern authority on the Ruwenzori, likens the giant lobelia to a sort of botanical big game. He notes that "they tend to appear in family groups,

Frequent rainfall in the Bujuku Valley supports luxuriant vegetation, including mosses and orchids.

and in the mist there is a curious anthropomorphism about them—they suggest extraterrestrial beings that will move as soon as one's back is turned."

Ruwenzori trekkers, their visual receptors unceasingly bombarded by the bizarre, may perhaps be excused a desire to fall into their tents at night and close their eyes, finally achieving respite from the supernatural. Fat chance. With the Ruwenzori night comes the weird shriek of the rock hyrax, a creature that looks rather like a large guinea pig but is zoologically a close relative of the

SUPERCOOL GARGOYLES

Because of the dense, almost constant cloud cover and barely subfreezing temperatures, ice accretes onto the upper crags of the Ruwenzori literally out of thin air. When supercooled water droplets of a cloud contact a solid surface, they condense as ice, in much the same way that ice builds up on airplane wings. Depending on wind, temperature, and cloud thickness, these tiny ice accretions build up over time to take on fantastic forms on the Ruwenzori summits: mushrooms, gargoyles, great overhanging buttocks and breasts, wind-pruned cauliflowers, hanging salamis, organ pipes, and delicate crystal flowers—a fantasy sculpture garden of ice.

Top: Porters cooking at John Matte hut, just below Lower Bigo Bog. Above: The "Mountains of the Moon," also called the African Alps.

brochures of trekking companies. For those seeking reassurance in the familiar, we'll close with some brochurelike, but still heartfelt words by the aforementioned Freshfield, a mountaineer of vast experience: "My impressions (of the Ruwenzori) are among the most vivid of a lifetime of travel. . . you may be familiar with the Alps and the Caucasus, the Himalaya, and the Rockies, but if you have not explored Ruwenzori, you still have something wonderful to see."

THE ROUTE

The jumping off spot for Ruwenzori treks is the hot, dusty, run-down town of Kasese. Trekkers actually begin walking at Nyakalengija, 13 miles from Kasese. The trail initially winds westward through grasslands and small farms up the lower Mubuku Valley, then ascends into the forest to the confluence of the Mubuku and Bujuku Rivers. You'll then proceed up the Bujuku Valley through the notorious Bigo Bog, a vast swamp where the mud is sometimes thigh-deep and trekkers must wear high rubber boots and hop from tussock to tussock. (In recent years, boardwalks have been constructed through some of the soggiest areas.) Once through the Bog, you'll pass Lake Bujuku, just shy of 13,000 feet and surrounded by the three main massifs of the Ruwenzori: Mounts Baker, Speke, and Stanley. You'll then turn south and climb to Scott Elliott Pass, at 14,300 feet the high point of the standard loop trail. (Spur trails lead to other huts as high as 16,000 feet, however.) Once over the pass, you'll descend to the Kitandara Lakes, loop around the backside of Mount Baker and descend the Mubuku Valley back to its confluence with the Bujuku, and thence retrace your steps back to Nyakalengija.

Some trek itineraries include various side hikes and climbs (with crampon, ice ax, and rope)

elephant. Patrick Synge, a young Cambridge naturalist who joined a 1934 British Museum expedition to the Ruwenzori, described the call of the hyrax as "gruesome shrieks and screeches which seemed to herald the approach of some monster, or the conversation of a party of prehistoric ghouls."

Ghouls, monsters, extraterrestrial beings—these are not words normally employed in the descriptions of mountains, particularly in the

Opposite: Stream crossing. Even in the dry season, rain and heavy mists are common. The rains create the snowpack on the main peaks, which in turn feeds the headwaters of the White Nile.

to the summits of one or more the three main mountains.

WHAT TO EXPECT

Because the Ruwenzori are so little traveled and densely vegetated, the usual rigors of high-altitude trekking—long days, steep climbs, thin air—are compounded by often poor footing on faint trails and occasional bushwhacking through dense growth. The word slog is often used to describe this arduous march. The camping is far more basic than what one might be accustomed to in Nepal, but the trek staff handles the load-carrying and camp chores.

The potential for rain and clouds makes this a stiffer mental challenge than other treks of comparable physical difficulty. The pioneering botanist A. F. R. Wollaston put it nicely almost a century ago: "The atrocious climate and the chance of seeing nothing once you get there will keep away all but the most determined and enthusiastic [trekkers]." Actually, it's not quite that bad; during the two brief trekking seasons (midsummer and midwinter), the clouds relent occasionally, and multiday stretches of fair weather are not unknown. But don't expect to come back with a tan.

Footing is wet and sloshy over much of the route. One Scottish trekker, a veteran of spongy bogs, reported that "the Ruwenzori make Rannoch Moor look like concrete."

Treks that include ascents of the peaks demand the full complement of basic moun-

IN 1906, FAMED ITALIAN EXPLORER and mountaineer, the Duke of Abruzzi, led the first large-scale expedition into the Ruwenzori, mapping the range and climbing all its major peaks. His photographer and friend, Vittorio Sella, captured this Bakonjo drummer on film.

taineering gear: crampons, ice axes, ropes and harnesses, as well as extra warm clothing.

GUIDES AND OUTFITTERS

As this book was being written in early 2000, the Ruwenzori area was closed to outsiders because of the unstable political situations in nearby Rwanda and the Congo (formerly Zaire). Prospects for its opening in the near future were uncertain. The Ruwenzori trekking service "industry" of guides and porters in Kasese has shut down, and of course no foreign outfitters offer trips at this writing.

Before the shutdown, independent trekkers had to work through Ruwenzori Mountain Service (RMS), a nonprofit organization in Kasese that maintained the trails and huts, supplied guides and porters, monitored the environmental impact of trekkers, and channeled trekking revenues into the local communities. RMS charged about $300 for the standard Ruwenzori loop trek described above, which it ran as a six-day trip, with no rest days, side hikes, or climbing forays. Presumably RMS will continue to be the focal point of Ruwenzori trekking once the area reopens. To check on the current situation, contact RMS.

RUWENZORI MOUNTAIN SERVICE
011-256-483-4115 (tel)
011-256-483-4235 (fax)
$300 for 6 days

A singular combination of copious rainfall, high elevation, low latitude, and moderate temperatures triggers in the Ruwenzori a botanical phenomenon called equatorial alpine gigantism.

Outfitters who say they plan to resume Ruwenzori treks once the area reopens include:

SHERPA EXPEDITIONS
011-44-181-569-4101
www.sherpa-walking-holidays.co.uk

WILD FRONTIERS
011-27-11-315-4838
www.wildfrontiers.com

RECOMMENDED READING

■ *GUIDE TO THE RUWENZORI,* Osmaston and Pasteur Written in 1972 and hard to get, but a mine of fascinating information nonetheless. An updated version is reportedly in preparation.

■ *UGANDA: THE BRADT TRAVEL GUIDE,* Phillip Briggs (1998. $17.95. Globe Pequot.) A British travel guide aimed at hikers and trekkers, with some good info on the Ruwenzori.

■ *AFRICA'S MOUNTAINS OF THE MOON,* Guy Yeoman History, biology, and geology leavened with personal anecdotes by a British expert adventurer.

■ *SNOWCAPS ON THE EQUATOR,* Gordon Boy and Iain Allen A coffee-table volume about Africa's equatorial peaks, including a chapter on the Ruwenzori. Excellent photos.

Ladakh: Across Zanskar

"... a high, arid valley...roosting ground for monks and yaks..."

"There were two atlases and one encyclopedia in the moraine of books that receding education had dumped in my household, and the word Zanskar appeared in none of them. That more or less settled things. . . .If neither the Hammond Atlas Company nor the Columbia University Press had ever heard of Zanskar, I wanted to go."

So mused writer/adventurer John Skow in a 1990 issue of *Outside.* A decade later, little has changed. Zanskar is still a place that hardly anyone has heard of, much less traveled to. Mention at a cocktail party that you have trekked across Zanskar, and you'll almost certainly get more raised eyebrows and quizzical looks than any other trekking destination in these pages would inspire.

Okay, so what and where is Zanskar? Skow again: "It (is) a high, arid valley in the Himalayas, . . .a roosting ground for monks and yaks, difficult

Trekker crossing an arid canyon in the remote, austere Zanskar Mountains of northwest India.

to reach and almost completely overlooked by travelers because it lacked both airstrips and paved roads. For centuries, Zanskar (has) been a separate, tiny kingdom, less familiar to the world than even Sikkim or Nepal. Now it was part of northern India, considered by the government, when it was considered at all, as a region of Ladakh. . . .Its people were Tibetan by race, language and their Buddhist culture. They were poor . . .but lived richly, in serene balance with their harsh environment. They welcome travelers with good humor and offer food and shelter without thought of reward. And their mountains. . . there were enough unclimbed and unnamed 6,000-meter peaks to keep (a mountaineer) busy for the rest of (his) life."

Yes, the mountains of Zanskar and Ladakh are splendid. But more remarkable still are the people, whose radiant contentment sometime stirs disbelief among cynical Westerners. By our economic standards, the Ladakhis are dirt-poor, the poorest people of India, with "incomes" of virtually zero. Yet they have achieved their own kind of material prosperity. A typical Ladakhi farm family works only about six months a year, yet manages to eat and dress well, live in a two-story 4,000-square-foot brick farmhouse, and still have enough excess wealth left over—crops or farm animals—to trade for silver, gold, and turquoise jewelry. How many people do you know who work six months of the year, live in 4,000-square-foot houses, and have lots of jewelry?

But perhaps more remarkable than the Ladakhis' materially comfortable lives—and even more to be envied by Americans— is their astonishing sense of joy and inner peace. "At first I didn't believe that the Ladakhis could be as happy as they appeared," writes Helena Nordberg-Hodge, a linguist who was the first Westerner in modern times to master the Ladakhi language, and who has studied Ladakhi culture since the 1970s. "Hidden behind the jokes and the laughter had to be the same (feelings of) frustration, jealousy and inadequacy as in my own society. . . .It took me a long time to accept that the smiles I saw were real."

Overleaf: Barley harvest at a remote village deep within Zanskar.

AT A GLANCE

TRIP LENGTH 28–31 days	PRICE RANGE (INDEPENDENT TREK) $500–$1,000
TIME ON TREK 17–22 days	PRICE RANGE (OUTFITTED GROUP TREK) $1,000–$3,500
WALKING DISTANCE 175 miles	
MAXIMUM ALTITUDE 16,900 feet	PRIME TIME July–August
PHYSICAL CHALLENGE 1 2 3 ④ 5	STAGING CITY New Delhi, India
MENTAL CHALLENGE 1 2 3 ④ 5	HEADS UP Recurring border clashes between India and Pakistan

Rope bridge along the trail from Manali (a staging outpost in Himachal Pradesh to the south) and Padam, in the heart of Zanskar.

"I have never met people who seem so emotionally healthy as the Ladakhis," Nordberg-Hodge continues. "Their contentedness and peace of mind do not seem dependent on outside circumstances, these qualities come from within. . . . A Ladakhi's identity is to a great extent molded by close bonds with other people, and is reinforced by the Buddhist emphasis on interconnectedness. People are supported in a network of relationships that spread in concentric circles around them—family, farm, neighborhood village. In the West we pride ourselves on individualism, but sometimes individualism is a euphemism for isolation. We tend to believe that a person should be self-sufficient, that he or she should not need anybody else."

"The closely knit relationships in Ladakh seem liberating rather than oppressive, and have forced me to reconsider the whole concept of freedom. Psychological research is verifying the importance of intimate, reliable, and lasting relationships in creating a positive self-image. . . .Ladakhis score very high in terms of self-image. It is not something conscious, it is perhaps something closer to a total absence of self-doubt, a profound sense of security."

Nordberg-Hodge sums it up this way: "The Ladakhis belong to their place on earth." It is a place we can visit, however briefly.

THE ROUTE

After a day or two of jet-lag recovery in the former hippie hangout (and current honeymoon haven) of Manali, trekkers start walking at Darcha, a dreary travelers' stop comprised mostly of tents. The first 7-to-11-day leg to Padam, the hub of Zanskar, crosses Shingo La, a 16,300-foot snow-covered pass ("Those sick can ride a horse," advises an old Indian guidebook) and then follows the Tsarap River on to Padam. Along the way you'll pass Phuktal Monastery, carved out of a limestone cliff. Just past Padam is Karsha monastery, Zanskar's largest. The 10-to-12-day second stage continues over 16,900-foot Shingi La to the 1,000-year old Lamayuru Monastery. From there you'll drive to Leh, the Ladakhi capital, and fly or drive back to Delhi.

The trek may also be done north to south, but since the best scenery is at the northern end, this option tends to be anticlimactic. Trekkers with limited time may do either the Karcha-Padam or Padam-Lamayuru stages, although the time saving is minimal due to the daunting logistics of getting to/from Padam by vehicle.

WHAT TO EXPECT

This is a rugged, remote, challenging trek. "You'll be out in the mountains for a very long time," says trekking guide Sanjay Saxeena of Geographic Expeditions. Most of the route is dry, arid country, with few villages. Those who trek on their own must be very well prepared, for trails are sometimes indistinct and there are limited supplies of food and fuel along the way.

Like Tibet, Zanskar is in the rain shadow of the Himalayas, untouched by the monsoon. Summer weather is generally good. In fact, after a couple of weeks you may grow weary of the brutal high-altitude sun (take plenty of sunblock and

Zanskari children attend school at a remote village. Zanskaris are supported in a network of relationships that spread in concentric circles around them—family, farm, neighborhood, village.

a good hat). Much of the time will be spent walking along relatively flat river valleys (even the valleys are high; you'll spend two solid weeks above 11,000 feet), but there are at least six passes above 12,500 feet that require steep climbs. Shingo La is usually snow-covered. There are also a number of interesting river crossings that require caution and expertise (always cross in the early morning, before mid-day snowmelt swells the river).

The 1999 flare-up of the long-running Kashmiri conflict reached Kargil, only about 60

YAK FIGHTS

The yak fights in Padam were first-rate. Yaks are vast, hairy, humpbacked beasts not much given to reflection. They are so dumb they can be parked like pickup trucks—they don't think to wander off. They do drift moodily about, however, and around midday the town square begins to fill up. The yaks would stand around sociably for a while, and then one, very slowly, would maneuver so that it was standing head-to-head with another. Each yak would then throw his hindquarters into low-low, and the stronger would push the weaker across the square. Or not: Sometimes the animals would forget what they were doing. No unseemly snorting or earth-pawing accompanied this drama. All was stately and serene. At the time, the yak fight seemed deeply symbolic, but I have since forgotten why.

—*John Skow*

A novice serves tea at a monastery.

sprung up along the route, there will be many nights when none is available. Bring along tent, sleeping bag, and plenty of food and fuel. It's usually possible to replenish your supplies in Padam, about halfway along the route, but be prepared for anything.

A guide is a virtual necessity; the trails are unmarked and can be confusing at times. Horses and horsemen can be arranged in Manali, Padam, or Leh. Cost is typically $5 to $10 per horse per day. (The horsemen in Manali, who have a strong union, are notoriously recalcitrant, finding any number of excuses to turn back at Shingo La.) As a general rule, hire guides and horsemen who live near your destination; the motivation of the homeward-bound is markedly higher.

LOCAL OUTFITTERS

There are local trekking outfitters in Manali and Leh. Reputable local outfitters charge $1,000 to $1,500 for the Zanskar trek. Leh outfitters are typically more reliable than those in Manali, a motivation to do the trek north to south. In Manali, ask for a recommendation at the Manali Institute of Mountaineering.

Larger Indian outfitters based in New Delhi also offer Zanskar treks. Indian Tribal Tours offers the trek in two halves. Padum to Darcha is $749; Padum to Lamayaru is $840. Treks start in Delhi and include all transportation and accommodations before and after the trek.

INDIAN TRIBAL TOURS
011-91-11-3723353 (tel)
011-91-11-3323906 (fax)
Email: ittindia@nda.vsnl.net.in

U.S. OUTFITTERS
At this writing, Geographic Expeditions and Himalayan High Treks are the only full-service U.S. outfitters we're aware of that run the

miles from Lamayuru. But rebel troops had withdrawn from the Kargil area by the time the trekking season arrived, so trekkers were generally not disrupted. In any case, Zanskar in particular and Ladakh in general are primarily Buddhist, so the Hindu-Muslim conflict in Kashmir has little direct impact.

GUIDES AND OUTFITTERS

It's possible to do the Zanskar trek on your own, but you must be very well prepared. "I've rescued more independent trekkers along this route than any other," says Sanjay Saxeena. Although a handful of Nepal-style teahouses (typically, somebody's spare bedroom) have

Monastery on the trail from Manali to Padam. A Ladakhi's identity is reinforced by the Buddhist emphasis on interconnectedness.

Zanskar trek described here. However, various other treks in Zanskar are available from several outfitters, among them Camp 5 Expeditions, Ibex Expeditions, Karakoram Expeditions, Snow Lion Expeditions, and Tenzing Travel.

GEOGRAPHIC EXPEDITIONS

888-777-8183
www.geoex.com
$3,445 for 31 days

HIMALAYAN HIGH TREKS

800-455-8735
www.himalayanhightreks.com
$3,100 for 32 days

RECOMMENDED READING

■ *ANCIENT FUTURES: LEARNING FROM LADAKH,* Helena Norberg-Hodge (1992. $12.00. Sierra Club.) A look at the impact of "progress" on the ancient Tibetan Buddhist culture that figured out long ago how to live the Good Life.

■ *A JOURNEY IN LADAKH,* Andrew Harvey (1984. $14.00. Houghton Mifflin.) One man's arduous spiritual adventure in the land of Buddhism.

■ *LADAKH: CROSSROADS OF HIGH ASIA,* Janet Rizvi (1998. $14.50. Oxford University Press.) The author is a western woman married to a Ladakhi.

■ *LEH TREKKING IN LADAKH,* Charlie Loram (1999. $16.95. Trailblazer Publications.) The most detailed trekking guide to the area.

■ *TREKKING IN THE INDIAN HIMALAYA,* Garry Weare (1997. $17.95. Lonely Planet.) Lonely Planet's walking guide, with a section on Ladakh and Zanskar.

The Milford Track

"After a while, paradise is numbing;
you grow satiated, drunk on prettiness..."

It all started with Sutherland Falls, a thundering 1,900-foot cascade that tumbles out of a mountain lake above Milford Sound, a 12-mile long fjord on the remote southwest coast of New Zealand. In 1880 Donald Sutherland, an eccentric hermit who lived on Milford Sound—the only resident of the three million acres of New Zealand's fjordlands—went on a prospecting expedition with a friend, John Mackay. The pair climbed through dense rain forest from Milford Sound up the Arthur River to a 3,800-foot pass. Along the way they spotted the spectacular three-leap falls, which they named after Sutherland by virtue of a coin toss. Carried away in their enthusiasm, they proclaimed the falls the highest in the world.

When word of Sutherland Falls got back to populated regions of New Zealand, a number of Kiwis—even then, dedicated hikers (or "trampers" in the local argot)—clambered to see this

Trekkers approaching 3,800-foot Mackinnon Pass, named for the Scotsman who built the Track in 1888.

SOUTH PACIFIC

*Milford
Sound*

● **Milford Sound**

*Fiordland
National
Park*

Clinton River

NEW ZEALAND
(SOUTH ISLAND)

natural wonder. And so in October, 1888 the local government commissioned the construction of a foot trail to the falls from the inland side, continuing on to Milford Sound via Sutherland's original route. Two months later, the first trekkers walked the 33-mile route, which came to be known as the Milford Track.

If not the most difficult, remote, or rugged trek described in this volume, the Milford Track is certainly among the oldest and most popular. Hundreds of thousands of people have walked it over the decades. Strictly controlled by the New Zealand government and featuring well-equipped hikers' lodges along its route, the Milford Track has managed to maintain its scenic magnificence and ambiance of isolation in spite of the tramping throngs and civilized amenities.

The novelist Bobbie Ann Mason hiked the Milford Track in the 1980s. A small-town Kentucky girl, she was bowled over by the visual splendor of New Zealand's fjordlands. "To describe the scenery on the Milford Track, one risks falling into a syrup of superlatives," she wrote in a 1989 issue of *Outside*. "This is beautiful scenery gone crazy. You can't take in the profusion of picturesque tree ferns, mossy trees, light-flecked beech forests, breathtaking waterfalls, rushing streams, stark mountain walls hiding the sun. After a while, Paradise is numbing; you grow satiated, drunk on prettiness. In 1908 the *London Spectator* described the Milford Track as 'the finest walk in the world,' and the title stuck. According to Maori legend, the goddess of the underworld was so alarmed at the beauty of the land—created by the god Tu-te-Rakiwhanoa—that she was afraid men who saw it would want to live there forever. To thwart this desire, she released a large *namu* (sandfly). Sand flies are the chief scourge of Milford Track trekkers, but I have a feeling their peskiness is exaggerated because there is little else to complain about. . ."

(Not everyone shares Mason's opinion, however; Captain Cook himself, cruising into nearby Dusky Sound in 1773 described the sand flies as "most mischievous animals that cause a swelling not possible to refrain from scratching.")

Much of the Milford Track's visual splendor is in the details, the small stuff. Mason was particular fascinated by the thick cushions of soft green moss that upholstered the landscape. Letting her household metaphors run wild, Mason wrote, "I

AT A GLANCE

TRIP LENGTH 8–10 days	PRICE RANGE (INDEPENDENT TREK) $200
TIME ON TREK 4 days	PRICE RANGE (OUTFITTED GROUP TREK)
WALKING DISTANCE 33 miles	$865–$925
MAXIMUM ALTITUDE 3,800 feet	PRIME TIME November–April
PHYSICAL CHALLENGE 1 ②③ 3 4 5	STAGING CITY Te Anau or Queenstown, New Zealand
MENTAL CHALLENGE ① 2 3 4 5	

Milford Track has maintained its magnificence and feeling of isolation in spite of its great popularity.

kept photographing moss, a shag carpet on a four-inch cushion. The tussocks of moss reminded me of those hooked rugs with raised, knobby designs, and the old-man's-beard moss hanging on everything made one think of slut's wool. . . . The tall mossy stumps. . .were like cat-scratching posts. . . . In places moss enveloped everything like plush-covered plumbing fixtures, and sometimes on rock walls moss dripped water like sopping-wet sponges. It was wall-to-wall beauty."

The high point of the Milford trek—we're talking elevation here, not necessarily scenery—is 3,800-foot Mackinnon Pass, named for the Scotsman who built the trail in 1888. As Mason describes it, "It's five zigs, six zags up to Mackinnon Pass. . . .When we reached (it) some-one shouted 'There's the can!' and I thought she meant the toilet, the Pass Hut Longdrop, built of concrete to keep it from blowing off the mountain, but it was just her New Zealand accent. She meant the cairn—the round rock memorial constructed in honor of Quintin Mackinnon. . . .The pass is wide, about 300 yards, and spotted with tarns (little lakes, what I personally would call ponds). . . .Sometimes it can be dangerously windy, and more often than not it's rainy and chilly. We could see forever in all directions. A woman in our party drove a golf ball off the

Opposite: Mitre Peak (c. 5,000 feet) towers over Milford Sound at the end of the Milford Track.

RAIN

Rainfall along the Milford Track averages 282 inches—that's 23.5 feet—a year. As Bobbie Ann Mason discovered, normal rain gear doesn't hack it. "The track officer who met our group at the Te Anau Resort Hotel scoffed at my Gore-Tex parka and insisted that I take a heavy yellow slicker from his stack in the office. . . .(He) said the yellow slicker weighed only half a pound, but in fact it weighed about 13 and a half pounds according to my shoulders on the morning of the first day. . . .Gore-Tex won't work when it really comes to rain, he insisted. There had just been severe flooding, stranding hikers on some other trails in the park. And my rubber overpants, although recommended gear in the trek brochure, wouldn't do to wade rivers. He told me to throw away those and my long canvas pants and thermal underwear. The proper costume, he informed the trekkers, is polypropylene long johns worn under shorts. The polypro keeps the legs warm even when you're fording streams and battling sudden storms. He said not to worry what you look like. . . ."

Crossing swollen Clinton River after a shower

edge of the pass with her walking stick. . .near Twelve-Second Drop, a big rock that juts out over the edge of the pass. Anything falling from there takes 12 seconds to hit the ground."

In case you're wondering, that works out to 2,304 feet.

Among the Milford Track's bewildering array of scenic wonders, Sutherland Falls—now relegated to merely the fourth-highest waterfall in the world—is still the main attraction. The falls are actually about a 45-minute walk from the main trail, but it is a mandatory diversion. Mason went one better by taking a scenic flight over the falls from the airstrip at Quintin Hut, the Track's most elaborate hiker lodge. "It would be hard to overstate how thrilling this ride was," she reports, "soaring on wings through the canyons, gliding over Lake Quill—which spills down over the mountain and creates Sutherland Falls. . .it was a calm clear day. Our wings caught the updraft, and we hung there in the air. . ."

Donald Sutherland could hardly have imagined it.

THE ROUTE

Most Milford trekkers start their journey in Te Anau, a small lakeside town a couple of hours south of the resort hub of Queenstown. Trekkers first take a bus along the shore of Lake Te Anau to Te Anau Downs, where they board a launch—the same boat that's been ferrying trekkers since

1899—for the ride to the end of the lake and the trailhead. From there you'll proceed across a swinging bridge over the Clinton River, then follow the river through thick beech forests up the West Branch into a waterfall-festooned canyon. The trail then ascends steeply to Mackinnon Pass, where, if the weather is good, there are great views of nearby peaks and lakes. As the trail descends the steep, narrow Roaring Burn, trekkers walk on wooden and metal stairways. A bit farther along is the side trail to must-see Sutherland Falls. The Track then descends along the Arthur River, skirting Lake Ada to Sandfly Point, the end of the Track. Here trekkers board a launch for Milford, then bus back to Te Anau or Queenstown.

WHAT TO EXPECT

This is among the most "civilized" treks in this volume. Because of its popularity, the New Zealand National Park Service strictly controls every aspect of the Milford Track. During the normal trekking season you'll need to reserve a permit well in advance, good for a specific departure day only. You must hike on a set itinerary, from south to north, taking four days and three nights—no more, no less—and staying in prescribed huts each night. Apart from the regimented atmosphere, the major downside of this controlled traffic flow is the lack of flexibility in case of bad weather. There is an upside, however: the route seems far less crowded than it really is (about 10,000 trekkers per year).

There are two distinct tiers of Milford trampers: "freedom walkers" and members of organized groups. The former carry their own food, cooking gear, and bedding and stay in a network of 40-bed basic huts (camping is not permitted along the Track). Group trekkers stay in more elaborate hotel-like huts with hot showers, beds, full dinner and breakfast menus—even beer and wine. Group trekker Bobbie Ann Mason described the meals as "enormous and practical. Breakfast included por-

Top: The trail follows the Clinton River through thick beech forests. Above: The launch Anita Bay *at Sandfly Point on Lake Ada, carries trekkers across the sound to Milford.*

ridge and bacon and eggs and toast and canned fruit and milk and Nestlés Milo (a powdered chocolate drink) and Nestlés Classic coffee and tea. (Down Under, 'Nestlés' rhymes with 'trestles.') The orange juice is like something astronauts would drink. And in New Zealand, they eat a concentrated yeast paste called Vegamite. They spread it on toast. . .with butter. It's said to repel sandflies because of the Vitamin B. The jars of Vegamite

In 1880 two prospectors, Sutherland and Mackay, on beholding the 1,900 cascade, proclaimed it the highest in the world. On a coin toss, they named it Sutherland Falls.

seemed to grow larger as we traveled farther into the bush."

Freedom walkers and group trekkers stay in different huts that are well separated. As a result, you'll see few other people, even though at any given moment some 300 trampers are on the trail.

The Track itself is carefully maintained, with many sections of boardwalk or wooden steps through the few difficult areas. Altitude is not a factor. Physically, this is an easy trek, suitable for kids as young as ten.

The weather can be a bit dodgy, however. The fjordlands are notoriously rainy, averaging almost an inch per day in December and January, the peak trekking months. Rain gear and a positive attitude are a must (see page 98).

KEA BIRDS

Unlike the jungles of nearby Australia, which abound with poisonous snakes and thorny, grasping vines, New Zealand's rain forests are benign and gentle. The most fearsome fauna along the Milford Track are the mildly annoying sand flies and an aggressive vandal called the kea bird. Mason writes, "At Pompolona Lodge. . .we were warned about the mischievous kea birds. They like to destroy hiking boots, picking out the eyes of the stitches, and they'll vandalize a room if they can sneak in a door. At dawn, they screech and slide down the tin roofs with bone-chilling sounds. They steal your food right out from under your nose. They're big birds with wicked-looking talons. Later in the trip, after finishing (the trek) we saw a little sports car convertible that had been stripped by keas—everything plucked bare, from upholstery to wiring to hubcaps."

GUIDES AND OUTFITTERS

Independent "freedom walkers," who travel on their own without guides, pay $60 for permit and hut fees, plus another $75 or so in bus and boat fares between Te Anau and the trailheads. Food brings the cost of the four-day trek to about $200.

As a member of a guided group, you'll carry a lighter pack, have the benefit of a guide to enlighten you about the local flora and fauna, and stay in plush hotel-like huts with hot showers and meals. The full package, including a night in a hotel in Te Anau before and after the trek, costs $925 for adults and $525 for kids 10 to 15. "Off-season rates (November and mid-March through April) are $865 and $485. In the tradition of Milford regimentation, there's only one authorized outfitter:

MILFORD TRACK GUIDED WALK
011-64-3-249-7411
$865–$925 for 6 days

The trip can also be booked through:
ADVENTURE CENTER
800-227-8747
www.adventure-center.com

RECOMMENDED READING

■ *TRAMPING IN NEW ZEALAND,* Jim DuFresne (1995. $13.95. Lonely Planet.) This Lonely Planet guide has a detailed route description of the Milford Track, as well as general info about the fjordlands region and New Zealand.
■ *CLASSIC TRAMPS IN NEW ZEALAND,* Constance Roos Ten pages on the Milford Track.
■ *THE SHELL GUIDE TO THE MILFORD TRACK,* Philip Temple Now out of print, this pocket-size pamphlet is part of a series of guidebooks to specific New Zealand tracks by a veteran Kiwi hiker/writer/photographer. Charmingly written, very detailed.

The Inca Trail

How else can you watch the sun rise over Machu Picchu?

He was the original Inca Trail trekker. In 1534, a 13-year old Spanish boy named Pedro de Cieza de Leon watched awestruck on the wharf at Seville as Francisco Pizarro's ship arrived from Peru, laden with the gold ransom of a kidnapped Inca emperor. His imagination fired, the boy soon embarked for the New World himself. For 17 years, Cieza traveled on foot and horseback, first as a soldier, then as an official chronicler, following The Royal Road of the Inca, the vast 10,000-mile network of stone-paved all-weather highways that stretched the length and breadth of the Inca Empire.

Like most trekkers, Cieza kept a journal—and what a journal it was! His eight-volume, 8,000-page chronicle touched on virtually every aspect of Inca civilization and its destruction by the Spaniards. Like any trekker, Cieza paid close attention to what lay underfoot. "A highway, built by man's hands and labor. . .left (Quito) and

The surefooted, generally gentle, sometimes inquisitive llama is the pack animal of choice in the Andes.

PERU

extended all the way to Cuzco, from there another began, as large and magnificent as this, which went to the province of Chile, which is more than 1,200 leagues from Quito." (A league is the distance a walking horse travels in an hour, about three miles.) The road ran ". . .over mountains so rough and dismaying that in certain places one could not see bottom, and some of the sierra so sheer and barren that the road had to be cut through the living rock to keep it level and the right width. All this they did with fire and picks. . ."

A surprisingly objective reporter, Cieza recognized the Inca highway system as far superior to anything in Europe. "I doubt there is record of another highway comparable to this, running through deep valleys and over high mountains, through piles of snow, quagmires, living rock, along turbulent rivers. . . .Everywhere it was clean-swept and kept free of rubbish, with lodgings, storehouses, temples to the sun, and posts along the way. Oh, can anything comparable be said of Alexander, of any of the mighty kings who ruled the world, that they built such a road. . .as this one! The road built by the Romans that runs through Spain, and the others we read of, were nothing compared to this. And it was built in the shortest space of time imaginable, for the Incas took longer in ordering it than their people in carrying it out."

"There were many of these highways all over the kingdom. Of all, four are considered the main highways, and they are those which start from the city of Cuzco, at the square, like a crossroads, and go to the different parts of the kingdom. . . . Nowhere in this kingdom of Peru was there a city with the air of nobility that Cuzco possessed, which was the capital of their empire and the royal seat."

A few remnants of those ancient Incan highways still survive, their cobblestones badly worn, but the artistry of their ingenious design and layout still intact. Among the best-preserved of all is a 35-mile section of the original winding cobblestone path between the former Inca capital of Cuzco and the fabled mountaintop shrine of Machu Picchu. The most renowned trekking route in South America, it has become known as the Inca Trail.

AT A GLANCE

TRIP LENGTH 8–13 days	PRICE RANGE (INDEPENDENT TREK): Not permitted
TIME ON TREK 4–5 days	PRICE RANGE (OUTFITTED GROUP TREK)
WALKING DISTANCE 35 miles	$200–$3,000
MAXIMUM ALTITUDE 13,650 feet	PRIME TIME March–November (mid-June through August
PHYSICAL CHALLENGE 1 2 ③ 4 5	is particularly busy. Trails will be crowded and you'll need
MENTAL CHALLENGE 1 2 ③ 4 5	a reservation for locally outfitted treks or guides).
	STAGING CITY Lima or Cuzco, Peru

Quechua men carefully balance loads on llamas in preparation for a trek.

It's not known whether Cieza ever trod this particular spur road out of Cuzco. But it's certain that neither Cieza nor any of his fellow conquistadors ever explored it to its terminus at Machu Picchu. That extraordinary cloud-swept citadel, the fabled Lost City of the Incas perched precariously on a mountaintop, surrounded by plunging canyons and even higher peaks, was not seen by a white man until 1911, when Yale archaeologist Hiram Bingham, acting on a tip from one of his Indian guides, slashed his way through the jungle to find it. In a subsequent expedition in 1915, Bingham and his crew, after many false starts and dead ends, managed to find and clear with machetes the faint traces of the section of road that trekkers walk today. "I found that it was good

enough for llamas and human burden-bearers," wrote Bingham of his discovery. "Wherever it followed a contour of a steep slope, it was banked up and supported by a stone wall. Where it had to climb a steep grade, stone steps were built with care so that the bearers of burden could be provided with secure footing. Finally, by a graceful curve, the road was brought to the top of the ridge and the city gate (of Machu Picchu)."

The origin and history of Machu Picchu are still a mystery. But perhaps the more intriguing riddle is this: How did such a large and magnificent site go entirely undiscovered by the Spaniards for 400 years? Geography was a major factor—"No part of the highlands of Peru is better defended by natural bulwarks," wrote

Opposite: Exploring the Incan ruins of Machu Picchu.

Main square of the old town of Cuzco. The four main highways of the Incan empire started from this square in the ancient capital city.

Bingham—but jungles and canyons alone could not have kept Machu Picchu hidden from the determined conquistadors.

Gary Ziegler, an archaeologist, trek leader, and Inca historian, has his theory. "The Lost City of the Incas wasn't really a city at all," Ziegler writes. "It was probably built by (the emperor) Pachacuti Inca as a royal estate and religious retreat in 1460 to 1470. Its location—on a remote secondary road in nearly impassable terrain high above the Urubamba River canyon cloud forest—almost ensured that it would have no administrative, commercial, or military use.

"After Pachacuti Inca's death, Machu Picchu remained the property of his *allus*, or kinship group, who were responsible for maintenance, administration and continued building. As an extraordinary sacred site, it surely was visited by Topa Inca and the last great ruler, Huayna Capac, although each in turn built their own estates and palaces. But few outside the (emperor's) retainers would have known of its existence.

"Of course the compound would have required a steady supply of outside goods. Machu Picchu, like most Inca sites, was undergoing constant construction and must have had a resident crew of builders as well as attendants, planters, and others."

So how was all this activity kept secret? "The Inca were a completely ordered, regimented society," writes Ziegler. "The royal roads were reserved for official travel. The Incas were able to control their remarkable state system through a pyramidal hierarchy (of) information. . . .We know from historical writing and the archaeological record that the Incas did not possess a written language, although, they must have used some symbols and perhaps diagrams. . . .The Inca maintained a class or guild of verbal historians. But with the catastrophic collapse of Inca state structure following the arrival of the Spanish, these historians were scattered and forgotten."

But other events may have blotted the memory of Machu Picchu even before the arrival of the Spanish to the Cuzco area. A smallpox epidemic around 1527 killed Huayna Capac and an estimated 50 percent of the Inca population. "Machu Picchu was probably abandoned at this time," writes Ziegler, "both because it was expensive to maintain and with most of the population dead from war or epidemic, it was hard to find the labor to keep it up."

The Pizarros didn't reach Cuzco until 1532. "The first wave of Spanish were mostly illiterate, uneducated adventurers," writes Ziegler, and they had little interest in anything

How did Machu Picchu go undiscovered by the Spaniards for 400 years? The origin and history of this ancient Inca mountaintop retreat may remain shrouded in mystery forever.

besides gold and plunder. "By the time scholars and administrators arrived, knowledge of Machu Picchu had been lost."

In 1536 the emperor Manco Inca staged an ill-fated rebellion against the Spanish. After his siege of Cuzco failed, Manco fled deep into the remote Vilcabamba mountains beyond Machu Picchu, destroying Incan settlements as he went to discourage Spanish pursuit. One of the towns he burned was Llactapata, where the abandoned royal road to Machu Picchu, by then badly overgrown, began climbing up from the Urabamba River. With the destruction of Llactapata (now a popular camping spot for Inca Trail trekkers), whatever chance the Spanish might have had of stumbling upon the old trail went up in flames.

THE ROUTE

From Lima, you'll fly to Cuzco, the "Kathmandu of the Andes." You should spend at least a couple of days here, partly because it's a fascinating place with many Inca ruins, and partly to acclimatize to the altitude. Elevation is 11,200 feet. You'll then take the popular tourist train from Cuzco toward Machu Picchu, but you'll get off at either Chilca (KM 77 on the train route), KM 82 or KM 88. The traditional starting point is KM 88, but Chilca is also a popular trailhead because it gives you an extra half-day walking along the river.

From Chilca, the usual first day is an easy half-day walk along the Urabamba River to Llactapata, the Inca town destroyed by Manco during his retreat to Vilcabamba. On Day 2, you'll leave the river and climb about 4,000 feet to Llulluchapampa. The trail then ascends to Warmiwanusqua ("Dead Woman's Pass") at 13,650 feet, the high point of the trek, and on down into the Pacasmaya Valley and the Runkurucay ruins. Then it's up over a second pass and along a particularly well-preserved section of road to the ruins at Sayacmarca. Finally, you'll

Trekkers stop for a tea break on the Inca Trail.

pass through an Incan tunnel, cross a third pass with more superb ruins, then head down a 1,600-foot flight of steps (discovered only in 1984), past a grim trekkers' hotel, and finally on to the glorious Intipunku, or Gateway of the Sun, where you'll get your first dramatic glimpse of Machu Picchu spread out below—surely one of the most dramatic vistas in the world.

From Machu Picchu, you'll train back to Cuzco and home.

WHAT TO EXPECT

Because it is not too difficult and easily accessible, the Inca Trail has become a mass-market trek. Machu Picchu itself is now a major tourist attraction. (There's talk of a cable car to the ruins that will vastly increase the current visitation of about 1,000 people per day.) Although as a trekker you'll definitely feel superior to the tourists who get to the ruins by train and bus, you won't feel like an explorer along the trail. In peak season, there are mad rushes for the best campsites. Locals sell trinkets. Robbers are not unknown along the trail, especially near the village of Huayllabamba.

Nevertheless, the extraordinary scenery and overpowering sense of history and spirituality make this a very special trek for many people, almost a pilgrimage. The famous first glimpse of Machu Picchu from the Gateway of the Sun will awe even the most jaded. For maximum effect, leave the trekkers' hotel—the last permitted camping spot before the Gateway—about two hours before dawn (don't forget your headlamp) and arrive at the Gateway just as the sun comes up.

GUIDES AND OUTFITTERS

At press time, Peru was poised to ban independent trekkers and backpackers from the Inca Trail, a measure deemed necessary to reduce crowding and environmental damage. For the latest on this situation, check with the South American Explorers Club in Cuzco at 930 Avenida del Sol (011-51-84-223-102; saec@wayna.rcp.net.pe). Or call their U.S. office at 607-277-0488.

LOCAL OUTFITTERS

There are dozens of local outfitters, however, and group treks leave every day during the season. Rock-bottom price is $150 (not counting your $50 trail fee) in which case you'll have tea and rice for dinner and probably carry some of your own gear. If you want a dependable English-speaking guide and good food and equipment, figure about $400 from Cuzco, or about $900 from Lima. Some of the top Cuzco outfitters are:

EXPLORANDES
011-51-1-445-0532
www.explorandes.com

ANDEAN TREKS
800-683-8148, and Tambo Treks

Several U.S. companies book the trips of the better local Peruvian outfitters. Try:

LATIN AMERICAN ESCAPES
800-510-5999
www.latin americanescapes.com

HIMALAYAN TRAVEL
800-225-2380
www.govp.com/himtravel.htm

ADVENTURE CENTER
800-227-8747
www.adventure-center.com

JOURNEYS INTERNATIONAL
800-255-8735
www.journeysinternational.com

SAFARICENTRE
800-624-5342
www.safaricentre.com

U.S. OUTFITTERS

A number of U.S. outfitters offer full-service Inca Trail packages, which typically include hotels in Lima, flights to Cuzco, and various side tours along the way. Some trips combine the Inca Trail with Galapagos tours, Amazon excursions, or other treks in Peru.

BRIDGE TO THE PAST

The vital sinews in the Inca system of Royal Roads were the *keshwa chacas*, or rope bridges, that spanned the vast river chasms in the high Andes. The Spanish chronicler Cieza reported seeing one bridge 250 feet long, 125 feet above the water, with cables "thick as a man's body" made from fibers of *cabuya*, a hemplike plant with spiny leaves. The bridge, approached through a tunnel on one side, was manned by a resident caretaker responsible for traffic control and maintenance.

After the fall of the Empire, some Incan rope bridges continued to be used and maintained by the local people—it was the locals who'd built them under orders from the Inca, after all—and a few lasted into the 20th century. (Thornton Wilder's short novel *The Bridge of San Luis Rey* focuses on one that finally collapsed in the 1890s.)

One Incan rope bridge still exists today, a 100-foot span across the upper Apurimac, an hour's drive west of the town of Yanaoca. Villagers say that their ancestors have maintained it continuously since Inca days. The annual reconstruction project requires four miles of finger-thin rope spun by village women and braided into cables by the men. The actual rigging of the bridge—starting with a single small "messenger line" nudged across the river's surface—takes 100 local men three days. All the while, offerings of corn and coca leaves smolder by the bridge's permanent stone cable anchors. Although there's a perfectly good steel cable suspension bridge a few hundred yards upstream, the villagers continue to perform this annual reconstruction rite as an affirmation of their cultural heritage.

Rutasha Adventures, a one-man travel company whose one man is retired Tennessee geology prof Ric Finch, runs a three-week trip to Bolivia and Peru that includes both the Inca Trail and a visit to the Apurimac rope bridge. His website is www.public.usit.net/rfinch/rutahsa.html, or call him at 931-526-1390.

ANDES ADVENTURES
310-395-5265
www.andesadventures.com
$2,350–$2,550 for 13-17 days (including airfare from Miami)

GEOGRAPHIC EXPEDITIONS
800-777-8183
www.geoex.com
$2,395 for 16 days

KE ADVENTURE TRAVEL
800-497-9675
www.keadventure.com
$2,395 for 14 days

MOUNTAIN TRAVEL-SOBEK
800-687-6235
www.mtsobek.com
$2,480–$2,780 for 13 days

REI ADVENTURES
800-622-2236
www.rei.com/travel
$1,995 for 10 days

SOUTHWIND ADVENTURES
800-377-9463
www.southwindadventures.com
$2,195 for 11 days

WILDERNESS TRAVEL
800-368-2794
www.wildernesstravel.com
$2,595–$2,895 for 15 days

RECOMMENDED READING

■ *LOST CITY OF THE INCAS: THE STORY OF MACHU PICCHU AND ITS BUILDERS,* Hiram Bingham The Yale archaeology professor who discovered Machu Picchu in 1911 tells the story of his expedition.

■ *THE CONQUEST OF THE INCAS,* John Hemming (1973. $22.00. Harcourt Brace.) Perhaps the best popular account of the rise and fall of the Inca Empire.

The Inca Trail seen through a window in the ruins of Huinay Huayna, well worth a side trip on the way to Machu Picchu.

■ *THE BRIDGE AT SAN LUIS REY,* Thornton Wilder (1998. $9.00. Harper Collins.) A short novel centered around one of the last remaining Inca rope bridges in the late 19th century.

■ *THE INCA TRAIL, CUZCO & MACHU PICCHU,* Richard Danbury The most up-to-date Inca Trail guide.

■ *PERU AND BOLIVIA: BACKPACKING AND TREKKING,* Hilary Bradt (1998. $17.95. Globe Pequot.) An excellent guide to the Central Andes, with a big section on the Inca Trail.

■ *EXPLORING CUZCO,* Peter Frost Covers the city and nearby hiking areas, including the Inca Trail.

Opposite: Quechua women. Nearly half of all Peruvians are Quechua-speaking, and most of them live in the highlands.

The Kanchenjunga Trek

"Go to Sikkim" a veteran trekker friend of mine whispered, as if revealing a great secret. "It's like Nepal was 30 years ago."

everybody knows that Mount Everest is the highest mountain in the world. Some people know that K2 is the second highest. But how many people can name the earth's third-highest peak?

Kanchenjunga, at just over 28,000 feet, lies astride Nepal's eastern border with the Indian province of Sikkim. No other great Himalayan peak can be seen so easily from a major population center (in this case, Darjeeling, India). For

that reason Kanchenjunga was believed to be the world's highest mountain until well into the 19th century. The great British mountaineer Eric Shipton described Kanchenjunga as "a far tougher proposition than either Everest or K2," and indeed the first attempt on its summit, led by famed occultist and mystic Aleister Crowley in 1905, failed miserably. No one got to the top until 1955, two years after Everest was first conquered. The first ascent from the Sikkim side did

Kanchenjunga, the earth's third-highest peak, lies astride Nepal's border with the Indian province of Sikkim.

not occur until 1977.

Americans typically know Sikkim, if they know it at all, as the tiny Himalayan Shangri-La whose king married a young American woman, Hope Cooke, in 1963. The real-life "King and I" fairy tale, alas, was ruined in 1975 when the then-autonomous kingdom of Sikkim was forcibly annexed by India, to be used as a buffer zone against arch-foe China, which borders it to the north. Happily, the region's Tibetan Buddhist culture has remained intact, and most local people, taking the long view, consider the Indian presence merely a temporary bureaucratic annoyance. The Indian government still doesn't allow individual foreign trekkers in Sikkim, and group treks are permitted along only a handful of approved routes.

But there's an upside to all this border paranoia: hardly any other trekkers. "Go to Sikkim," a veteran trekker friend of mine whispered, as if revealing a great secret. "It's like Nepal was 30 years ago." Okay, Kanchenjunga isn't Everest, but for this visual peak-bagger, a sacrifice of two slots on the tall mountain pecking order seemed a small price for a 30-year hiatus in the encroachment of Western civilization.

The goal of our Sikkim trek was Goecha La, a 16,400-foot pass in the shadow of Kanchenjunga with dramatic close-up views of the peak. Our trip leader, Daku Tenzing Norgay—a smiling, vivacious Nepali woman of a certain age, and the widow of famed Everest summiteer Tenzing Norgay—met us in the foothill city of Darjeeling at the Windamere Hotel, a gloriously seedy hilltop relic of bygone British elegance, and, incidentally, the place where Hope Cooke was first introduced to the King of Sikkim. Tall for a Nepali woman, with a stately bearing and long black hair pulled back tightly into a braid, Daku had smooth skin, perfect teeth, and a raucous deep-bellied laugh. I adored her at once.

The next morning—my first in the Himalayas—a few of us arose before dawn and walked to an overlook near the Windamere to watch the sunrise. Mist obscured the view to the east, but through a break in the clouds to the north we suddenly glimpsed the summit of Kanchenjunga, some 50 miles away. I gasped in astonishment. To one whose scale of reference is

AT A GLANCE

TRIP LENGTH 17–21 days	PRICE RANGE (INDEPENDENT TREK) Not permitted
TIME ON TREK 9–10 days	PRICE RANGE (OUTFITTED GROUP TREK)
WALKING DISTANCE 75 miles	$600–$3,600
MAXIMUM ALTITUDE 16,400 feet	PRIME TIME April–May, October–November
PHYSICAL CHALLENGE 1 2 ③ 4 5	STAGING CITY Delhi, India
MENTAL CHALLENGE 1 2 ③ 4 5	HEADS UP Relations between India and China can effect travel safety

Rice terraces, Nonli, a small village about 30 miles south of Gangtok, Sikkim, India.

the Rockies and Alps, it seemed preposterous that rock and ice could float so far above the horizon.

We departed by Land Rover for Gangtok, Sikkim's airportless capital city. From Gangtok, we continued through steep green valleys to Pemyangtse, site of Sikkim's most revered Buddhist monastery, where we got another dawn view of Kanchenjunga's four-summited massif. But the mountain disappeared behind the ridgetops as we drove on to the village of Yoksum, the literal end of the road.

The first two days of trekking took us rather steeply up a lush valley of oak, spruce, magnolia, and rhododendrons. Kanchenjunga still lay frustratingly out of sight behind the steep ridges. At our first night's camp, we were entertained by our trek crew's futile attempts to deal with one particularly recalcitrant pack animal. (We were using *dzos,* surefooted yak/cow hybrids whose great arcing horns belied their usually placid demeanor.) This particular *dzo* was anything but placid, and at one point fomented a *dzo* stampede that nearly flattened my tent, with me inside it. Daku christened it the Naughty *Dzo.*

On the morning of the third day we crested a knoll to see Kanchenjunga once again, this time looming much closer. Our camping spot that night, a lovely meadow called Dzongri, was a special place for Daku. It was here, as a 15-year-old porter, that she first caught the eye of her husband-to-be, Tenzing, then the training director of the Himalayan Climbing Institute. Born at 15,000 feet in Nepal, the unschooled daughter of a yak herder, Daku had run away from home at the age of 13 to escape an arranged marriage. Taking along 60 rupees (about $1.20) and four young friends in similar premarital straits, she walked through the mountains for 18 days to Darjeeling.

She married Tenzing in 1959, when she was 17 and he 45. Because of his mountaineering renown, they traveled the world together and knew many famous people. But her life was not easy with the hard-drinking Tenzing, and she longed for the high places. "I always feel better out in the mountains," she told me. "At home there are many problems. The lower you go, the more you have to think about." She had no interest in remarrying. "Once is enough. I don't like to be squeezed in my life."

At Dzongri, our tents lay below a steep grassy knob that jutted up 1,000 feet and promised superb views of the Big One, as we'd come to call Kanchenjunga. I organized a predawn mission to climb the nob to once again watch the first rays of the sun light the summit. Three bleary-eyed recruits and I started climbing in darkness and reached the top in the first faint glow of dawn to find a row of Buddhist prayer flags waving gently in the breeze. We sat mute among the whispering flags, the snowcapped peaks towering around us, as the sky brightened. None of us was particularly religious, but when the summit of Kanchen-junga suddenly turned golden, we all agreed that if indeed there were a God or Buddha or whatever, he (or she) was probably not far from this time and place.

From Dzongri, we hiked up a broad valley, past yak herders and piles of prayer-inscribed *mani* stones. Five days out from Yoksum, we finally pitched our tents at Jemathang, next to a holy lake at 15,750 feet, the jumping-off spot to our final goal, Goecha La. Once again we rose before dawn, this time in hopes of reaching the pass before midday clouds obscured the summit. The altitude and rough, rocky terrain turned back

Novice monk at Rumtek Tibetan Buddhist monastery near Gangtok.

three of the group, but 11 of us pressed on through the barren landscape. Traversing one last tricky snow-covered slope, we arrived at the pass just as the first wisps of cloud began to stream from the summit looming above us.

As prayer flags whipped in the bitter wind, Daku picked up a stone and added it to a ceremonial pile. She then burned an offering of incense branches, sprinkling rice, nuts and seeds into the fragrant flames. We had conquered a mere pass, not a summit, but we felt thankful to the mountain gods all the same.

Top: The Windamere Hotel in Darjeeling.
Above: A jeep is not necessarily any less recalcitrant than a dzo, the yak/cow hybrid pack animal.

THE ROUTE

From Delhi, trekkers typically fly to Bagdogra, then drive about 60 miles into the Himalayan foothills to the old British hill station of Darjeeling. Most commercial treks include visits to Kalimpong, Gangtok, and Pemyangtse before finally reaching the trailhead at Yoksum. From there, it's a five- or six-day walk up a well-established trail to Goecha La, then three or four days back to Yoksum.

WHAT TO EXPECT

This is a typical Himalayan trek, with six to eight hours of hiking each day along trails that can occasionally be quite steep. (Yes, the camp staff hews to the Nepal tradition of waking clients each morning with hot tea in their tents.) Altitude ranges from 6,000 to 16,000 feet. The push to Goecha La is the most challenging part of the trip, but since it's an out-and-back route, the weary or footsore may elect to stay in camp for the day.

Don't expect much culture or local color along the trail. Although the trailhead village of Yoksum is an intriguing little place, there's only one other small village along the trail, on the first day. For most of the trip, you'll see only mountains and the occasional yak herder. When

A DRUMMING TO DARJEELING

The drive from Bagdogra to Darjeeling will take you along a twisting mountain road that in most places is not wide enough for two large vehicles to pass. As a result, whenever your bus meets an oncoming bus or truck, it must back up to one of the few wide spots in the road. (If the closest wide spot is ahead of you, the other guy has to back up. Don't worry about arguments; the drivers know all the wide spots by heart.) To aid in the intricate backing-up maneuvers, a second crewman is employed to signal the driver when the way is clear behind. The lookout, who stands on the rear bumper, communicates to the driver by banging on the side of the bus in a steady drumbeat of code. Bop-BOP bop-BOP means "plenty of room, keep going." Bop-BOP means "enough room, proceed with caution." A succinct BOP means "you're going to hit something pretty soon." No bops at all means "stop."

Young monks eating lunch, Tibetan chorten in Gangtok.

I made the trek in 1990, a stroll along the main street of Yoksum triggered a stampede of curious kids. Nowadays visitors are not such a novelty —though Yoksum is still a far cry from the Khumbu and Annapurna areas of Nepal, where foreign trekkers sometimes outnumber the locals.

Before and after the trek, however, you'll be immersed in Tibetan Buddhist culture in Gangtok and at various monasteries. And Darjeeling, a teeming hilltop city that has few roads but vast networks of footpaths, will keep you culturally entertained for as long as you care to stay.

GUIDES AND OUTFITTERS

Independent trekking is not allowed in Sikkim. You must sign up with an outfitter and travel in a group of at least four.

LOCAL OUTFITTERS

In Gangtok and Darjeeling local outfitters can arrange Kanchenjunga treks that typically run 12

Base camp at 16,900 feet, only 500 feet above Goecha La, the author's goal on his Kanchenjunga trek.

to 14 days and cost $600 to $1,000. (In comparing prices with American outfitters, remember that the U.S. company typically provides transportation to and from, and lodging in Gangtok or Darjeeling.) In Gangtok, Sikkim Trekking and Travel runs a 12-day Goecha La itinerary with a special permit. Another recommended Gangtok outfitter is Tashila Tours and Travel (Fax 011-91-3592-22155).

SIKKIM TREKKING AND TRAVEL
Fax 011-91-3592-22707
email sikkimtrekking@mailcity.com
$660 (each)/4 people; $900 (each)/2 people

U.S. OUTFITTERS
American outfitters typically run variations of

the Goecha La itinerary. Mountain Travel-Sobek, which organized my Sikkim trek, currently runs virtually the same itinerary under the leadership of Jamling Tenzing Norgay, the son of Daku and Tenzing. (Sadly, Daku died of a mysterious intestinal ailment in 1994, during a pilgrimage to Nagaland in eastern India.) Jamling has become something of a celebrity in his own right after starring in David Breashears' 1998 IMAX Everest movie.

A small company called TrekSikkim also offers the Goecha La trek with a celebrity-offspring angle. The trip leader, and company co-founder, is Hope Leezum Namgyal, the daughter of the former King of Sikkim and Hope Cooke (yes, that makes her a princess).

KE Expeditions offers an itinerary that

HEAVENLY BUDDHA

On a wall in the library of the 450-year old Pemyangtse Monastery is a huge painting of 1,000 Buddhas. Each is identical except for slight variations in the position of their hands.

If that's not surreal enough for you, up on the third floor is an exquisitely detailed seven-tiered model of the imaginary heavenly abode of the Buddhist deity Padmasambhava. We were told that the model, about 12 feet high and sporting rainbows, angels, and uncounted Buddha figures, took three monks eight years to build.

includes the Goecha La route plus a six-day trek along the Singalila Ridge, which straddles the Sikkim/Nepal border south of Kanchenjunga. Worldwide Adventures runs a 19-day Goecha La trip that includes five days in Bhutan, starting in Calcutta and ending in Kathmandu. Other listed outfitters offer the standard unadorned Goecha La route.

ADVENTURE GUIDES INTERNATIONAL
www.adventureguidesintl.com
$3,295 for 18 days

GEOGRAPHIC EXPEDITIONS
800-777-8183
www.geoex.com
$3,145 for 18 days

HIMALAYAN KINGDOMS
011-44-117-923-7163
$3,550 for 20 days

KE EXPEDITIONS
800-497-9675
www.keadventure.com
$3,195 for 21 days

MOUNTAIN TRAVEL-SOBEK
888-687-6235
www.mtsobek.com
$3,540 for 21 days

TREKSIKKIM
212-996-1758
www.gorp.com/rareearth/wildindia/sikkim/about
$3,400 for 17 days

WORLDWIDE ADVENTURES
800-387-1483
www.worldwidequest.com
$2,250 for 19 days

RECOMMENDED READING

■ *TIME CHANGE*, Hope Cooke A first-person account of life in the Sikkimese monarchy by the American woman who married the King
■ *TREKKING IN THE INDIAN HIMALAYA*, Gary Weare (1997. $19.95. Lonely Planet.) Lonely Planet's walking guide, with a chapter on Sikkim.

PORTERS, SIKKIM, 1899. Famed Italian mountaineer and photographer Vittorio Sella was official photographer for British explorer Douglas Freshfield's 1899 expedition to Kanchenjunga. They reached as far as 20,200-foot Jonsong-La Pass.

■ *EXPLORING THE HIDDEN HIMALAYA*, Mehta and Kapadia A complete history of mountaineering on Kanchenjunga and surrounding peaks.
■ *ABODE OF SNOW*, Kenneth Mason A history of Himalayan exploration and mountaineering, including Kanchenjunga.

The Haute Route

Two weeks of nonstop "Heidi" in the birthplace of mountaineering.

Among the many storied peaks of the Alps, two stand above the rest: Mont Blanc (literally), at 15,781 feet the highest mountain in the Alps—indeed, in all of Western Europe—and the Matterhorn (figuratively), the graceful 14,691-foot pyramid whose jutting summit, perhaps the most recognizable in the world, has become the aesthetic mountain ideal.

So it was inevitable that somebody would try to devise a walking route linking the two Alpine icons, their summits stand just 38 miles apart. In 1861, a group of climbers from the Alpine Club of Britain were the first to accomplish this feat. Their "High Level Route" wound more than 100 miles through the most rugged and remote region of the Alps, from the French town of Chamonix, at the foot of Mont Blanc, to Zermatt, the Swiss village in the shadow of the Matterhorn.

By the turn of the century, skis had become the rage. French and Swiss skiers began to make

The Matterhorn, near Zermatt, Switzerland, with Riffelsee *(Riffle Lake) in the foreground.*

the traverse in early spring, translating the Britishers' name for the walking path as "Haute Route." Over the next few decades, the Haute Route was known primarily as a ski trip, and it is still a classic among ski mountaineers. But with the growth of trekking, the walker's Haute Route has made a comeback—albeit in milder form, at lower altitudes that avoid most glacier crossings.

For all its height and history, Mont Blanc is visually bland, a broad, fat mountain whose summit is well out of sight of Chamonix. The Matterhorn, by contrast, towers dramatically over Zermatt. For this reason, most Haute Route trekkers choose to walk west to east, from Chamonix to Zermatt, with the Matterhorn serving as their visual and mental homing beacon. Edward Whymper, the first man to climb the Matterhorn, in 1865, walked the final section of what is today's Haute Route into Zermatt a number of times, and he described the arrival this way: "The tourist toils up the valley, looking frequently for the great sight that is to reward his pains, when, all at once, as he turns a rocky corner of the path, it comes into view; not, however, where it is expected; the face has to be raised up to look at

it—it seems overhead."

By contrast, Whymper dismissed the charms of the Mont Blanc Range. "It attracts the vulgar by the possession of the highest summit of the Alps. . . .It has not the beauty of the Oberland."

When Whymper first arrived in Zermatt in 1861, the Matterhorn ". . .was the last great Alpine peak that remained unscaled—less on account of the difficulty of doing so, than from the terror inspired by its invincible appearance. There seemed to be a cordon drawn around it, up to which one might go, but no further. Within that invisible line, djinns and effreets were supposed to exist—the spirits of the damned. The superstitious natives in the surrounding valleys. . .spoke of a ruined city on the summit where the spirits dwelt; and if you laughed, they [the natives] gravely shook their heads; told you to look yourself to see the castles and the walls, and warned one against a rash approach, lest the infuriate demons from their impregnable heights might hurl down vengeance for one's derision." (Those who dismiss the vengeance of Matterhorn demons do so at their peril; on the descent after the triumphant first ascent of the mountain in 1865, four

---

AT A GLANCE

TRIP LENGTH 12–16 days	**PRICE RANGE (INDEPENDENT TREK)** $700–$1,000
TIME ON TREK 10–14 days	**PRICE RANGE (OUTFITTED GROUP TREK)**
WALKING DISTANCE 110 miles	$2,000–$2,600
MAXIMUM ALTITUDE 9,700 feet	**PRIME TIME** July–September
PHYSICAL CHALLENGE 1 2 ③ 4 5	**STAGING CITY** Chamonix, France
MENTAL CHALLENGE 1 ② 3 4 5	

Trekkers near Chamonix in the French Alps.

members of Whymper's seven-man expedition were killed when a rope broke.)

Although Whymper never walked the complete Haute Route, he covered portions of it. While crossing the Col de la Forclaz, a pass along the route near the village of Triente, Whymper complained that he was ". . .persecuted by trains of parasitic children. These children swarm there like maggots in a rotten cheese. They carry baskets of fruit with which to plague the weary tourist. They flit around him like flies; they thrust the fruit in his face, they pester him with their pertinacity. Beware of them! Taste, touch not their fruit." The 21st-century trekker is unlikely to encounter such annoyances. And who is to say that profferings of fruit might not in fact be welcome?

The final stage of the trekking route, from Zinal to Zermatt, leads a wildly roundabout course to skirt a rampart of high peaks and icy passes that lie between the two villages. When Whymper found himself in Zinal in 1864, he decided to thrust straight into this unexplored wilderness to find a more direct route to Zermatt. After spending the night in a "hovel. . . surrounded by ordure and dirt of every description" owned by a "foul native," Whymper's party set off into the teeth of the mountain gauntlet. The weather was atrocious, but "the idea of vegetating in the foul den for another 24 hours was too fearful to be entertained."

The going was rougher than Whymper had anticipated. Of the traverse of one particularly treacherous ice slope, he later wrote, "The peril

SWISS GUIDES

Swiss mountain guides have a reputation as the best in the world. And why not? They live in the place where mountaineering and mountain guiding were invented 150 years ago, and their qualifying standards are high and strictly enforced. The phrase "Swiss Guide" has become synonymous with disciplined competence.

So why did I have such a rotten time on my two excursions with Swiss guides?

The first was a climb of the Allalinhorn, a modest snow-covered peak above Saas Fee, a ski resort near Zermatt. Our guide was a fit-looking guy in his 60s named Otto, highly recommended by the mountaineer-

ing shop where I rented my crampons. Not having used crampons in a couple of years, I was momentarily unsure of the proper strapping pattern, and asked Otto for some help. He sneered contemptuously, called me a spoiled baby in German (he didn't realize I understood what he was saying), and brusquely showed me which strap went where.

One of my fellow climbers, a German guy who was a complete novice, somehow managed to get his crampons on backwards. Otto either didn't notice or

continued on page 124

Opposite: The Matterhorn's instantly recognizable 14,691-foot summit.

continued from page 123

didn't care enough to point out the error. It wasn't until we were well under way that a passing climber noticed the German guy's problem and quickly set things right. Where was Otto during all this? Several hundred yards ahead.

After a couple of hours, we stopped for a rest. I pulled out my water bottle and raised it to my lips, only to have Otto swat it away. He grabbed it out of my hand and pretended to throw it over a cliff. "Don't drink water," he told me sternly. "Very bad for you." Now I am not exactly Sir Edmund Hillary, but I do know that drinking lots of water is one of the most important things a climber or trekker can do. A mountain guide who tells a client not to drink water is like a driving instructor who advises his student to drive 100 mph on the left side of the road. From that moment on, I stayed as far away from Otto as possible. Needless to say, he didn't get a tip.

Three years later, I was a journalist visiting a high-altitude medical research facility on the summit of Monte Rosa, at just over 15,000 feet the second-highest mountain in the Alps. (There's a great view looking down at the Matterhorn.) A group of scientists and I were led to the top by a young Swiss guide. Now this fellow was at least competent. But despite the fact that we had plenty of time, he set a blistering pace that left me and most of the rest of the party—roped together for safety—gasping and floundering. One fellow kept shouting from the back of the rope, begging for a slower pace, but our guide would hear none of it. Soon thereafter, on a gentle down-hill section during which we were virtually running in our crampons, the man tripped and fell, jerking the team to a halt. Although I managed to avoid tripping, what should have been a wonderful climb was needlessly transformed into a grim ordeal.

Perhaps I have been spoiled by American guides. Their attitude—with a few exceptions—seems to be

"I'm here to get you to the top, keep you safe, and do everything I can to help you have a good time. " The Swiss Guide's attitude seems to be "I am here to demonstrate my superiority over you. I want to get this over as quickly as possible, so I am going to go very fast. If you can't keep up, we'll have to turn back due to your incompetence. Too bad you aren't a great climber like me."

The legendary Alpine mountaineer Edward Whymper seems to back me up here. Before he found his stalwart guide Michel Croz, a Frenchman from Chamonix, "My experience with guides (at the Matterhorn) had not been fortunate," he wrote in 1871. One group of self-proclaimed guides he described as "a series of men. . .whose faces expressed malice, pride, envy, hatred, and roguery of every description." One local Matterhorn guide he did hire on several occasions, an accomplished mountaineer named Jean-Antoine Carrel, ". . . was conscious that he was indispensable to me, and took no pains to conceal his knowledge of the fact. If he had been commanded, or if he had been entreated to stop, it would have been all the same." On one occasion Carrel failed to show up for a planned attempt to climb the Matterhorn with Whymper. The day had dawned a fine one, so Carrel went hunting instead. Whymper later noted, "An incident like this goes far to make one look favorably upon the (guides) of Chamonix."

Nevertheless, Whymper hired Carrel for what turned out to be his successful first summit of the Matterhorn in 1865. But Carrel had ambitions of his own to be the first to climb the Matterhorn, and secretly agreed to lead another group of climbers up the Italian side of the mountain instead, leaving Whymper in the lurch. In a delicious bit of irony, Whymper and his hastily assembled team reached the top while Carrel's party was 600 feet below the summit. Whymper kicked down a few rocks to make sure Carrel realized he'd been beaten to the prize. (In a final irony, the two later made up and climbed together for years all over the world.)

was obvious. It was a monstrous folly. A retreat should have been sounded." But it wasn't. Led by the fearless French guide, Michel Croz, the party reached the safety of solid ground seconds before a massive pinnacle of ice "as high as the Monument at London Bridge" crashed down the slope they had just crossed. Sobered, the party pushed on nevertheless, traversing more knife-edge ridges, passes, and glaciers before arriving at the Monte Rosa Hotel in Zermatt just before dark.

Modern trekkers will not encounter monument-size blocks of falling ice. But they will immerse themselves in the same extraordinary mountain scenery that drew Whymper and other pioneering climbers year after year. "The ablest pens have failed, and I think must always fail, to give a true idea of the grandeur of the Alps," Whymper wrote. You're right Ed. I'm not even going to try.

THE ROUTE

The classic Haute Route Begins in Chamonix, at the foot of Mont Blanc, and crosses a long series of north-south ridges and valleys, ending at Zermatt in the shadow of the Matterhorn. The route occasionally follows roads or ski lifts, and regularly dips into valley towns and villages. This allows hikers to "cheat" occasionally—or bail out altogether—if legs or spirits falter.

A number of variations and alternative routes for certain stages are possible, but the best guidebook for the Haute Route, by Kev Reynolds, suggests the following itinerary: From Chamonix, proceed to the nearby town of Argentiere, then cross the border (and a modest pass) to the Swiss town of Trient. The route then passes through the villages of Champex and Le Chable, makes a long climb to Mont Fort hut, and then crosses three high passes and the Grand Desert Glacier to Prafleuri Hut. From there you'll descend to the picturesque mountaineering village of Arolla, to La Sage, up to Moiry hut, down to the village of Zinal, and on to the Hotel Weisshorn, a splendid Victorian relic that stands a thousand feet above the valley. You'll then pass through the villages of Gruben and St. Niklaus before finally marching wearily up the valley to Zermatt, with the Matterhorn looming dramatically above. (Don't you dare take the train or the bus on this last leg!)

WHAT TO EXPECT

Essentially, this is two weeks of nonstop *Heidi*. The Alpine scenery is of course outrageous—it is, after all, the landscape that has defined what mountains look like for generations of Europeans and Americans. (You think the Paramount movie logo is modeled after the Rocky Mountains? Think again. It's right there

Above: "...a massive pinnacle of ice 'as high as the Monument at London Bridge' crashed down the slope..."

Aiguilles de Chamonix (the Chamonix needles) reflected in Lac Blanc, east of the Chamonix Valley.

in front of you on the last day of the trek.)

Culturally, the Haute Route may be the only trek in this volume—with the possible exception of the Dolomites—during which the American trekker will feel inferior to the local population. (How does it happen that this unprepossessing Swiss village is what Vail has spent a couple of billion dollars trying to be? Why don't we have mountain huts like this back in the States? How do they get it together to keep these trails so well maintained and signposted?) The one word that perhaps best describes the Haute Route trekking experience is. . .civilized.

GUIDES AND OUTFITTERS

You don't need a guide to do the Haute Route, but you do need a good map and guidebook. Although Swiss trails are well marked, there is no signed "Haute Route" as such. You have to know where

you're going. Mountain huts typically cost $25 to $30 per day, including breakfast and dinner, while village hotels range from $75 to $100, meals included. Figure perhaps $1,000 for the full 14-day trek—less if you're willing to slum it in the villages and seek out a hostel or *dortoir* (a place to throw down a sleeping bag under a roof). Reservations are advised for both huts and village hotels. You may occasionally have trouble persuading village hoteliers, accustomed to guests who stay a week or more, to accept you for just one night.

LOCAL OUTFITTERS

Chamonix, the starting point, is perhaps the world's premiere mountain sports town, so there is a huge selection of local guides and trekking operators. The best resource is the guides' organization, La Compagnie des Guides de Chamonix (011-33-45-053-0088).

U.S. OUTFITTERS

American trek operators also offer Haute Route trips that cover all or part of the route.

BILL RUSSELL'S MOUNTAIN TOURS
800-669-4453
www.russelltours.com
$2,295 for 14 days

CAMP 5 EXPEDITIONS
800-914-3834
www.camp5.com
$2,490 for 12 days

DISTANT JOURNEYS
888-845-5781
www.distantjourneys.com
$2,195 for 13 days

MOUNTAIN TRAVEL-SOBEK
888-687-6235
www.mtsobek.com
$2,490 for 10 days

PENNY PITOU TRAVEL
800-552-4661
www.pennypitoutravel.com
$2,100 for 10 days

WILDERNESS TRAVEL
800-368-2794
www.wildernesstravel.com
$2,495–$2,595 for 13 days

RECOMMENDED READING

■ *SCRAMBLES AMONGST THE ALPS*, Edward Whymper (1996. $13.95. Dover.) The classic 1871 work describes the Alpine exploits of the man who first climbed the Matterhorn and explored many of the passes and peaks encountered by Haute Route walkers.

■ *CHAMONIX TO ZERMATT, THE WALKER'S HAUTE ROUTE*, Kev Reynolds The Haute Route trekkers' bible, with detailed route description and accommodations listings for each stage. If you're an independent trekker, don't leave home without it.

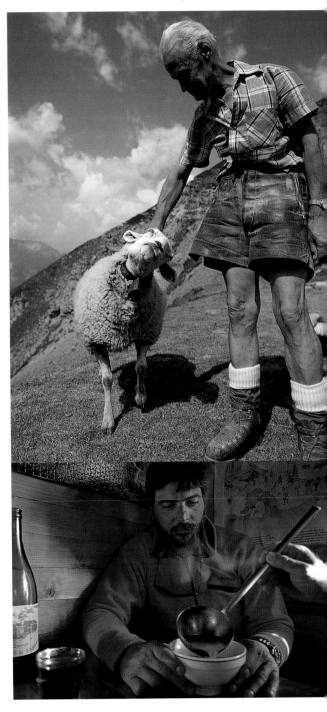

Top: French trekker on the Haute Route revisiting sites he had seen serving in World War II. Above: A climber enjoys dinner at Valsorey mountain hut.

The High Atlas

In its combination of mountain scenery and intriguing local culture, the Atlas ranks right up there with the Himalayas and Andes.

Pliny, the great Roman geographer, described the Atlas Mountains of Morocco as "the most fabulous mountains in all of Africa." He was wrong. But give the guy a break. Kilimanjaro and the Ruwenzori weren't discovered by white people until a couple of thousand years later.

It's indisputable, however, that the Atlas are the most fabulous mountains in North Africa. A swath of rugged peaks arcing a thousand miles from the Mediterranean to the Atlantic, the Atlas have been inhabited for 4,000 years by Berber tribesmen who have tenaciously held to their cultural independence. In the face of wave after wave of invasion of the surrounding lowlands by various ancient empires—and some modern ones as well—they have clung to their language and most of their ancient ways. (The Berbers' one concession to the outside world was the adoption of Islam in the seventh century.) In its combina-

Along the route from Marrakech to the High Atlas, whose snowcapped peaks are just visible in the distance.

MOROCCO

Marrakech

HIGH ATLAS

ALGERIA

tion of mountain scenery and intriguing local culture, the Atlas ranks right up there with the Himalayas and the Andes.

The heart of the Atlas range is the High Atlas. The lofty peaks, snow-covered most of the year, loom over the city of Marrakech, whence they've long lured European adventurers. One of the earliest High Atlas trekkers was C. E. Andrews, an intrepid British professor who set out from Marrakech in 1921 accompanied by a French friend, Monsieur Lapandery; Little Kbira, an eight-year old Berber girl adopted by Lapandery; and a local guide, Si Lhassen. Andrews describes Si Lhassen as "a most amusing oaf, good-natured and quite useless, with no interest in anything but food." For all his colonial arrogance, however, Andrews at least realized that the cultural gap ran both ways; he writes that Si Lhassen looked at him in return "as though I were some curious variety of beetle, and his expression seemed to say, 'Isn't Nature wonderful!' "

French colonial authorities had forbidden Andrews to enter the Atlas because of the danger of attack by fierce Berber tribesmen. Andrews was unfazed. "The decision did not deter us; we had expected it. We were going without permission. . . ." Led by Si Lhassen, with mules carrying supplies, the expedition left Marrakech and headed up the valley of the Nifs River, the next watershed west from the most popular present-day route into the mountains. "The first adventure in the dangerous forbidden zone was the cordial, hospitable reception of a Berber mountain man," Andrews noted sarcastically. "He followed us two miles trying to persuade us to be his guests at his mountain hut." Andrews was eventually persuaded to have a spot of tea with the man. "The little family group was extremely poor. . . they had but a handful of tea and a little sugar, but the cordiality and gracious courtesy of our host was the most complete in the world." This traditional Berber hospitality is still evident today; in villages along the trails, trekkers are often invited in to sip mint tea.

But Andrews and his party soon ". . .ran into an adventure which came near bringing the expedition to a sudden and fatal end." While letting their mules eat from a pile of straw near an abandoned hut, Andrews was smugly smoking a pipe and "making scornful remarks about the French

AT A GLANCE

TRIP LENGTH 15 days
TIME ON TREK 10 days
WALKING DISTANCE 75 miles
MAXIMUM ALTITUDE 13,700 feet
PHYSICAL CHALLENGE 1 2 ③ 4 5
MENTAL CHALLENGE 1 2 ③ 4 5

PRICE RANGE (INDEPENDENT TREK) $300–$600
PRICE RANGE (OUTFITTED GROUP TREK)
$600–$3,000
PRIME TIME May–September
STAGING CITY Marrakech, Morocco

Wheat harvest, crossing the High Atlas from Marrakech to Ouarzazate.

authorities with their fear of native hostility. . . . At just this moment, a very ugly head with a savage scar over the jaw popped up in front of us. In a minute two more heads appeared, and shortly (we were) completely surrounded by eight Berbers armed with rifles and long, brass-sheathed *poignards*. They closed about us in an angry circle, all hoarsely shouting at once and gesticulating with clenched fists. . . .Evidently we were in a predicament."

It was eight-year old Kbira who saved the day. Translating the Berbers' shouts, she explained to Andrews that the abandoned hut was in fact a sacred marabout's shrine, and the straw had been left there under the protection of Allah. To disturb the straw was a grievous sacrilege. With Kbira translating—and smiling—the ignorant infidels explained they had meant no harm, that they too were men of God who would not knowingly affront another religion. Overcome by Kbira's charms, the Berbers grudgingly allowed them to leave.

But Andrews' luck soon ran out—or did it? Near the village of Aoulouz, they called at the palace of a local Berber chieftain. Upon discovering that his unexpected visitors had no

Opposite: Mountain village near Tizi n'Test pass in the western High Atlas.

Berber boy in front of Glaoui Kasbah, a traditional North African home.

authorization papers, the chief promptly put Andrews' party under house arrest. There they languished for eight days in a luxurious ennui, waited upon by Abyssinian slaves.

"Time. . .ceased to have any significance, and had become a succession of dreaming moments," noted Andrews, reflecting an oft-cited phenomenon among trekkers as they recede farther and farther from their normal "civilized" lives, their minds floating free during long hours of putting one foot in front of the other. "As the peaceful days. . .wore on, amid quaint scenes of strange, quiet beauty, we gradually fell into the. . .calm desuetude which is the ideal of the older world." The calm of the east is not the dull placidity of Holland, or the inane vacuous torpor of the American Sunday mood, with its conscious virtue in acquiring merit by imposed leisure; but rather the calm of beatitude, the acceptance of peace as the normal state of the soul. . . .I used to wonder what profound mysteries, what deep truths of life old bearded Arabs pondered as they sat for hours, their backs against the wall and their eyes turned

KIDS, DON'T TRY THIS AT HOME
PART I

The convoluted infighting among Berber tribes and their various Islamic sects has been remarkable for its ingenuity and cruelty. Consider the 12th-century exploits of Ibn Tumart, founder of the Almohad dynasty, as reported by the British journalist Budgett Meakin in his 1899 book *The Moorish Empire*:

"After a battle. . .in which he was defeated with serious loss, (Ibn Tumart) went at night to some of his surviving followers and buried them alive, with only a hole through which to breathe, inducing them to submit to this process by the promise that if they would inform any who made inquiry that they were enjoying in Paradise the rewards of death in conflict with the infidels, he would disinter them, and allot them important posts. Returning with his disheartened supporters, Ibn Tumart remarked upon the good fortune of those who had fallen in battle, adding that if they had any doubts, they should go and ask the dead themselves. . . .They went to the gravesides and shouted, 'Oh dead companions, tell us what you have received from God Most High.' One can imagine their surprise when gladsome voices from the very earth assured them of a present state of bliss. . .Ibn Tumart's cause was revived, but as dead men tell no tales, return of fortune was denied his accomplices, whose breathing holes (Tumart) filled up after lighting fire over them."

At the neighborhood well, village along route to the High Atlas.

inward. I suspect now that they think of nothing. And I have become just like them. Life is merely a succession of faintly perceived sounds and shadows, and now and then comes couscous and tea. That is all!

"And so perhaps I have come to a true understanding of life, and perhaps the orientals are right in just letting it float by."

THE ROUTE

Starting at Marrakech, you'll drive a couple of hours to Asni, and then on to Imlil, a pleasant farm town along the Mizane River that has become the jumping-off spot for most High Atlas treks. From Imlil, the most popular route by far is the short two-day ascent of Jebel Toubkal, at 13,672 feet the highest mountain in North Africa.

There are myriad choices for longer treks, but one 10-day loop has become a semi-classic. This trek starts with a climb east out of the Mizane Valley, down across the Imanane River and then up to Oukaimeden, a winter ski resort that is virtually abandoned in the summertime. (There is a phone, and a good hut operated by the French Alpine Club.) Then it's back down to the riverside village of Tacheddirt, up and over another ridge to a Berber camp at Likempt, then over yet another pass to Amsouzart, a village on the Tifinout River that actually boasts a refrigerator. From there you'll climb to Ifni Lake, the only lake in the Atlas, and proceed to the Toubkal Refuge to rest up for the ascent of Toubkal itself. After an optional climb of nearby Ouanouk-rim—not quite as high as Toubkal, but more scenic and with less annoying scree—

you'll descend back to Imlil.

A hundred miles to the east of Toubkal is the second-highest peak in the Atlas, Jebel Mgoun. There's good trekking around Mgoun, and several of the outfitters listed offer treks in this area as well. A third Atlas trekking hotspot is Jebel Sahro, a region of low-lying foothills between the high peaks and the Sahara. More arid and less populated, with wild and dramatic rock formations, Jebel Sahro is a good place to trek in the winter, when snow blocks the main High Atlas trails.

WHAT TO EXPECT

This is not a wilderness experience. There are well-maintained mountain huts at key locations, and trails are much trodden by locals. Typically, you'll pass several villages a day. In those respects, the Atlas is much like Nepal: a beguiling combi-nation of geography and local culture. The weather is hot and dry, with pleasantly cool nights.

The trails are occasionally steep, but altitudes are, for the most part, modest. The valleys typically lie at 6,000 to 7,000 feet, with ridgetop passes at 9,000 to 10,000 feet. You'll huff and puff, but altitude maladies like pulmonary and cerebral edema should not be a problem.

Trekkers expecting the Berber trek staff and villagers to display the extraordinary friend-liness and good cheer of the Sherpas in Nepal will be disappointed. "They don't naturally have as much of the milk of human kindness," comments one veteran British Atlas guide. Although hos-pitable to a fault, many Berbers tend to have what one guidebook calls "a highly developed sense of survival." Another guidebook, less euphemistic, calls them "greedy." These opinions reflect the

KIDS, DON'T TRY THIS AT HOME
PART II

Joseph Thomson, an early explorer of Morocco, re-ported the following encounter with an Aissawa— a Muslim snake charmer—during his 1888 expedition into the High Atlas:

"For a moment he held the (snake) aloft by the neck, man and reptile staring fixedly at each other, as if trying to decide which had the superior power of fasci-nation. While we still wondered what was to be the next move, he suddenly raised the snake to his mouth. A vicious snap and the snake was headless, though it still wriggled in unceasing convulsions. With incredible rapidity, the snake's head was chewed and swallowed. Our disgusted protest was unheeded, as rigid, with eyes fixed. . .the Aissawa next bit off several inches from the body of the snake. . . . The poison was coursing through his veins, and he was in the fell clutches of delirium. . .he threw himself prone on the earth and on all fours jumped about with brutish gestures and wild animal howls, gnashing the ground with his teeth. . . .A more strange or sickening scene it would be difficult to imag-ine. . . .All at once he sank to the ground paralyzed, moaning and quivering as if in his death throes. . . . Finally the Aissawa looked up. His eyes wore a softer expression, though the foam still rested about his mouth. . . .The deadliness of the poison had been over-come. . . .With one voice the Moors acknowledged the greatness and omnipotence of Allah.

"An hour later (as the Aissawa sat near the campfire), he drew forth from the center of the glowing embers a piece of charcoal, held it—I will not say coolly —between the tips of his fingers while he blew it to a white heat, then he calmly put into his mouth, and leisurely munched, then swallowed, with evident signs of enjoyment, while the Moors broke into cries of 'Allah Akbar!' (God is great!) Apparently, the Aissawa had eaten his dinner first and was cooking it afterwards."

A mountain village in the Tizi n'Tichka region of the High Atlas, between Marrakech and Ouarzazate.

Western view of the time-honored Berber tradition of haggling over money. To a Berber, haggling is as natural as the sun and the moon. An American sees it as aggressive selfishness and intimidation. Try to remember: it's just business. Nothing personal.

Also, be prepared in Marrakech for the harangues of aggressive self-proclaimed guides, who want to steer you through the souk (marketplace) or to other tourist sites. This pestilence against foreigners has been brought under control to some degree in recent years, but the obnoxiously persistent "guides" are still a major bummer for any foreigner.

Fortified hill town in the High Atlas.

GUIDES AND OUTFITTERS

Morocco is a short plane ride from most European capitals, and the base of the High Atlas peaks is only a couple of hours drive from Marrakech. This easy accessibility has made the High Atlas exceedingly popular among British, French, and German trekkers.

In well-trodden areas like Toubkal, there's a good trekking infrastructure, and the independent trekker will have no problems finding transport from Marrakech, or hiring guides and/or mules in Imlil, the jumping-off spot for Toubkal treks. (Imlil, incidentally, was transformed in 1996 into a Tibetan village for a few days by Martin Scorsese, who filmed scenes from his feature film *Kundun* there.) The *Bureau des Guides* in Imlil has a list of several dozen accredited guides; figure on paying one about $15 to $20 a day, plus a tip of one day's wages at the end of the trek. A mule to carry your stuff (along with its muleteer) is about $8-$10 per day. A number of villages along the trail have basic trekker lodgings or mountain huts ($4 to $6 per night), but if worse comes to worst, you can always sleep out under the stars; rain is rare during the summer trekking season.

LOCAL OUTFITTERS

Group treks with local outfitters are easy to arrange in Marrakech. Backpacker hangouts like the Hotel Ali and Hotel Foucauld can arrange them, and have bulletin boards with ads from local companies. Figure on $40 to $60 per day for basic treks.

U.K. AND U.S. OUTFITTERS

A number of British outfitters run Atlas treks, with numerous departures at good prices. These treks may be booked in the U.S. through designated American agencies, but for the best pretrip information, we'd suggest contacting the British outfitters directly.

EXODUS
011-44-181-673-0859
www.exodustravels.co.uk
U.S. agent: GAP Adventures
800-692-5495
$735–$1,035 for 15–22 days

EXPLORE WORLDWIDE
011-44-125-231-9448
U.S. agent: Adventure Center
800-227-8747
www.adventure-center.com
$425–$525 for 15 days

SHERPA EXPEDITIONS
011-44-208-572-97880
www.sherpa-walking-holidays.co.uk/
U.S. agent: Himalayan Travel
800-225-2380
www.govp.com/himtravel.htm
$1,175 for 15 days

In addition, the following U.S. outfitters operate their own full-service Atlas treks—although not necessarily the itinerary described here—which typically include side trips and city tours of Marakkech and/or Fez.

IBEX EXPEDITIONS
800-842-8139
$2,195 for 18 days

MOUNTAIN TRAVEL-SOBEK
888-687-6235
www.mtsobek.com
$2,590–$2,990 for 15 days

WILDERNESS TRAVEL
800-368-2794
www.wildernesstravel.com
$2,295–$2,395 for 15 days

RECOMMENDED READING

■ *THEIR HEADS ARE GREEN AND THEIR HANDS ARE BLUE*, Paul Bowles (2000. $14.00. Norton.) A series of essays about the Sahara and North Africa.

■ *LORDS OF THE ATLAS*, Glavin Maxwell Classic account of the rise and fall of a Berber mountain clan in the early 20th Century. At one point, this book was banned in Morocco.

■ *THE ATLAS MOUNTAINS, A WALKER'S GUIDE*, Karl Smith A British guidebook that is up to date and long on detailed trail info, but woefully short on good maps.

■ *MOROCCO*, Frances Gordon et al. (1998. $17.95. Lonely Planet.) Lonely Planet's guidebook has a section on High Atlas trekking, as well as good info about Marrakech.

The Mount Kailas Circuit

"... in some mysterious way Kailas seems to have the power to touch the spiritual side of man..."

In the mind of a mere human being, a mountain can trigger mystery, fear, humility, hope, and something approaching divine inspiration. So it is no surprise that the concept of the "sacred mountain" is widespread in human culture. Dozens, if not hundreds, of summits around the world are seen as divine in some way: Fuji, Sinai, Kanchenjunga, Ararat, Olympus, Popocatapetl, Arunchala, Chomolhari, Machupuchara—even Everest itself, known to Tibetans as Chomolungma, or Mother Goddess of the World.

But a good case can be made that the most revered mountain on the planet is Mount Kailas, an exquisitely chiseled 22,028-foot pyramid that juts out of the arid high plains of western Tibet. Kailas is held sacred by no less than four religions: Buddhism; Hinduism; Jain, an Indian offshoot of Buddhism; and Bon, an ancient Tibetan animist cult that predates Buddhism by several centuries and still has a number of adherents. Although the

Pilgrimage to Mount Kailas, known to Tibetans as Mother Goddess of the World.

TIBET
(CHINA)

Mount
Kailas

Lake
Manasarovar

INDIA

Simikot

NEPAL

tally of pilgrims that flock to Kailas pales in comparison to say, Fuji, their ardor does not: The typical Kailas pilgrim walks 200 or 300 miles round trip, crossing the entire Himalayan range twice, for the privilege of making the *kora*, the ritual 33-mile circling of the mountain that cleanses all past sins and brings true enlightenment. (The walk must be made clockwise, with the mountain always off your right shoulder—unless you're a practitioner of the contrarian Bon faith, in which case you go counterclockwise.) Certain particularly zealous devotees make the entire circuit while prostrating themselves, inch-worm style, an ordeal that can take up to 25 days. Writes Kailas historian John Snelling, ". . .in some mysterious way Kailas seems to have the power to touch the spiritual heart of man; in the past this has been as true for hard-headed explorers as it has for the more impressionable pilgrims."

What sort of mountain is this that inspires such devotion? For one thing, Kailas is uncannily symmetrical, a nearly perfect pyramid that rises dramatically above the surrounding hills and rolling high plains, visible in its lone splendor from many miles away. "Such is the regularity of the mountain that it looks as though it might have been carved by human—or more accurately, superhuman—hands," writes Snelling. The Kailas area is also the source of four of Asia's great rivers: the Brahmaputra, Indus, Karnali, and Sutlej, which radiate from it like rays from the sun. This geographical oddity is probably the most convincing evidence that Kailas is the inspiration for the mythical Mount Meru, the centerpiece of Buddhist and Hindu cosmology that also is the source of four cosmic rivers and rises 84,000 *yojanas* high. (Sorry, nobody seems to know just what a *yojana* is.)

For trekkers, Kailas has always carried the allure of the unknown and the forbidden. It is exceedingly remote, 900 desolate miles west of Lhasa by a wretched dirt road, guarded on the south by the main Himalayan Range and the north by the Taklamakan Desert. For centuries, Tibet's xenophobic rulers banned all outsiders from entering the country. (For a time, any local chieftain who allowed a foreigner to slip

---

AT A GLANCE

TRIP LENGTH 23–31 days
TIME ON TREK 10 days
(two segments: 4 and 6 days)
WALKING DISTANCE 75 miles
(two segments: 33 and 42 miles)
MAXIMUM ALTITUDE 18,600 feet
PHYSICAL CHALLENGE 1 2 3 ④ 5
MENTAL CHALLENGE 1 2 3 4 ⑤

PRICE RANGE (INDEPENDENT TREK) Not permitted
PRICE RANGE (OUTFITTED GROUP TREK)
  $2,500–$7,500
PRIME TIME May–June, September–October
STAGING CITY Kathmandu, Nepal
HEADS UP Logistical uncertainty, Chinese border guards, and altitude demanding

across the border would be executed.)

Fittingly, the first Westerners to see Kailas, in 1715, were men of the cloth, a pair of Jesuit missionaries. Passing by on their way from Ladakh to Lhasa, one of them noted that ". . .owing to snow on the mountain, my eyes became so inflamed that I well nigh lost my sight." Western eyes did not again gaze upon Kailas until 1812, when a British official of the East India Company, William Moorcroft, disguised himself as a Hindu pilgrim and walked 100 miles across the Himalayas to check out possible trading opportunities. His goal was not Kailas, but nearby Lake Manasarovar, a sacred lake in its own right, and at 14,950 feet the world's highest large body of water. Although Kailas is plainly visible from the vicinity of the lake, Moorecroft mentioned the mountain only in passing, noting that if indeed Kailas were the throne of the Hindu god Shiva, "as its summit is always sheathed in clouds, it is but a cool seat." Moorecroft himself was on the hot seat a few weeks later when, trying to sneak back through Nepal without permission, he was arrested. After intense questioning, he was eventually released back to India.

The first substantial Western visit to Kailas occurred in 1846—a small party of British commandos on a spy mission to ferret out Russia's influence and intentions in Tibet. Its leader, Lt. Henry Strachey, raved, "In picturesque beauty, Kailas far surpasses any of the Indian Himalayas I have seen. It is full of majesty, a king of mountains." In the following decades a handful of British hunting parties invaded the Kailas area, defying local authorities, slaughtering wild yaks, and committing such spiritual atrocities as sailing an inflatable boat on Lake Manasarovar, a sacrilege for which the local *dzongpan*, or Buddhist headman, was held responsible and subsequently beheaded.

In 1904 Sir Francis Younghusband led a large British Army force to Lhasa and essentially intimidated the Tibetans into opening up diplomatic relations and allowing foreigners to enter the country. In 1907, the Swedish explorer Sven Hedin became the first Westerner to circumambulate Kailas in the manner of so many pilgrims before him. "At every turn, I could stand still in astonishment," he rhapsodized, "for this. . .is one of the grandest and most beautiful wildernesses I have ever seen." Coming from Hedin, who had probably seen more of Central Asia than any man alive, that was no small endorsement.

During his ritual walk, Hedin found a succession of monasteries along the circuit ("set like precious stones in a bangle."), meditation caves, and ceremonial rock towers, or *chortens*. He encountered the *dipka-karnaks*, testing-stones for sinners that contained narrow passageways; squeeze through them, and you're certified sin-free. (Hedin, a large man by Tibetan standards, declined the test, but, disconcertingly, one of his

Opposite: Pilgrim traveling to Mount Kailas. Above: Tibetan prayer carved into glacier-polished granite on the pilgrimage route around Mount Kailas.

servants got stuck.) Near the high point of the circuit, the 18,600-foot pass called Dolma La, he saw a huge boulder on which pilgrims traditionally smeared butter and then affixed something of themselves—typically, a tooth. (A photograph taken a few years later shows dozens of human teeth wedged into crevices of the boulder.) Modern trekkers need not fear for their molars, however; a lock of hair or an item of clothing will suffice in these less rigorous times.

As Hedin discovered, when it comes to diversions along the trail, no trek compares with the Kailas circuit. "There are literally thousands of holy sites along the route," says Gary Loth, a trekking guide (and erstwhile Buddhist monk) who's been to Kailas twice. "Virtually every step of the way, there's something."

THE ROUTE

This is an unusual trekking route that involves

NO GUTS, NO VAINGLORY

For sheer audacity and me-bwana-you-scum arrogance, few have matched the vainglorious blowhard British adventurer A. H. Savage Landor, whose 1897 expedition to Lake Manasarovar and Mount Kailas is a tale of extraordinary hardship and fortitude—if you believe it. Savage Landor played the role of colonial overlord to the hilt, cuffing and kicking uncooperative Tibetan peasants, and even forcing one to literally lick his boots.

Like many of his predecessors to Kailas, Savage Landor disguised himself as a Hindu pilgrim, and he was particularly adept at avoiding, ignoring, defying, or duping Tibetan authorities. When one threatened him with instant beheading if he set foot across the border, Savage Landor scoffed, "I paid little attention to these intimidations." Later confronted by 30 armed Tibetan soldiers on horseback, Savage Landor's expedition made a show of turning back, but A. H. himself immediately doubled back toward Kailas with a few trusted coolies. Traveling at night to avoid detection, he reported in his book *In the Forbidden Land* that he ". . .naturally had escapes and adventures far too numerous to relate here in detail. . ." One that he did relate in some detail was his alleged (but much doubted) discovery of the source of the Brahmaputra River, now known as the Tsang-Po.

But Savage Landor eventually got his comeuppance when he and his two servants were captured by a large Tibetan force in a struggle that he claimed lasted 20 minutes. Unrepentant to the core, he later wrote, "When I realized that it took the Tibetans 500 men. . .to arrest a starving Englishman and his two half-dying servants, and that even then, they dared not do it openly, but had to resort to abject treachery; when I found that these soldiers were picked troops from Lhasa and Shigatze despatched on purpose to arrest our progress and capture us, I could not restrain a smile of contempt for those into whose hands we had fallen."

He was then forced to ride several miles on a "torture horse" equipped with a spiked saddle. "I pretended not to feel the effects of the spikes tearing the flesh off my backbone; and when they led me to the Pombo to show him how covered in blood I was, I expressed satisfaction at riding such an excellent pony. This seemed to puzzle them."

Further threats of torture were made, to which A. H. says he merely laughed. Finally, a swordsman/executioner appeared and took two sweeping blows at Savage Landor's neck, each missing by a half-inch, customary preludes to the fatal third stroke. But the Pomba interceded at the last second, and a gloating A. H. and his terrified servants were taken to a border town and allowed to escape. He later described the execution ceremony as ". . .very picturesquely carried out. . . performed with extra pomp and flourish. . .really impressive."

two distinct trekking segments and a grueling five-day drive between Kailas and Lhasa, the Tibetan capital. Trekkers first fly from Kathmandu to Nepalgung, and then Simikot, in far western Nepal. From Simikot, trekkers walk six days through the mountains to the Tibetan border. From there, they drive in Land Cruisers about 50 miles north to Lake Manasarovar, and then on to Kailas for the four-day cirumambulation. Then comes the long difficult drive to Lhasa. After sightseeing in Lhasa, the trip finishes with a flight back to Kathmandu.

Some outfitters make the trip in reverse, starting with the drive from Lhasa and trekking out through Nepal.

WHAT TO EXPECT

This a very rugged, and unpredictable trip, among the most adventurous in this volume in terms of logistical uncertainty. You're virtually guaranteed to get stuck on the road between Lhasa and Kailas (wheel-sucking phenomena include mud, sand, snow, river crossings, and landslides). Your guides will probably have to bribe the imperious and capricious Chinese border guards, or at least get them drunk. (A few groups have even been turned back, despite having all the proper permits.) Outside Lhasa, tourist facilities of any kind are nonexistent or depressingly primitive.

The five-day drive between Kailas and Lhasa can be a real drag, especially for active people unaccustomed to being cooped up in a jouncing vehicle hour after hour. To make matters worse, the vast landscape along the route for the most part lacks diverting details—although it is undeniably breathtaking when taken in its entirety.

The ambiance along the trail around Kailas, however, stands in dramatic contrast to its spare, forbidding setting. "It's a county fair atmosphere," reports Effie Fletcher, whose company runs regular Kailas treks. "Families having picnics, playing games. Most of the people along the route are

Brahmaputra River. The Kailas area is the souce of four of Asia's great rivers, including the Indus.

very jovial, and happy to include us in their rituals and games. Even the yaks look festive, with their red ribbons, which signify that they've made the *kora* and therefore can never be slaughtered."

Altitude is a very serious matter on this trip; you'll spend three weeks above 12,000 feet, and almost two weeks at 15,000 feet or more. But, according to Swami Pranavananda, author of *The Pilgrim's Companion to the Holy Kailas and Manasarovar*, "Any person who has not got very weak lungs or affected heart" is physically capable of doing the pilgrimage. (Of course, it helps to live at 13,000 or 14,000 feet, as many Kailas pilgrims do.)

GUIDES AND OUTFITTERS

Independent trekking is forbidden by the Chinese authorities.

LOCAL OUTFITTERS

A number of Kathmandu-based outfitters offer the above itinerary or variations thereof. Check the Visit Nepal Network (www.VisitNepal.com or 011-977-1-416239) for a listing of outfitters. A typical program is offered by Getaway Himalayan Eco Treks, which offers an 18-day Kailas trek that bypasses Lhasa altogether and completes the Kailas circuit in a brisk 3 days before trekking back to Simikot (depending on group size).

GETAWAY HIMALAYAN ECO TREKS
011-977-1-424-921
www.visitnepal.com/getaway/welcome/html
$2,500–$3,500 for 18 days

U.S. OUTFITTERS

Several American outfitters offer turnkey trips out of Kathmandu, with extensive side trips and tours. Noteworthy is that of Wilderness Travel, which adds an eight-day round-trip trek to the source of the Indus, following in Sven Hedin's footsteps.

HIMALAYAN HIGH TREKS
800-455-8735
www.himalayanhightreks.com
$5,000 for 31 days

KE ADVENTURE TRAVEL
800-497-9675
www.keadventure.com
$4,100 for 23 days

SNOW LION EXPEDITIONS
800-525-8735
www.snowlion.com
$5,300 for 27 days

WILDERNESS TRAVEL
800-368-2794
www.wildernesstravel.com
$7,595 for 38 days

A New Zealand outfitter worth noting is Footprint Tours, run by John and Diane McKinnon, longtime Nepal residents and compatriots of Edmund Hillary. Their website is a mine of information on Mount Kailas.

FOOTPRINT TOURS
011-643-545-0145
www.greenkiwi.com.nz/footprints
$5,600 for 30 days

RECOMMENDED READING

- *THE SACRED MOUNTAIN*, John Snelling (East West Publications.) An excellent history of Kailas, written in 1983, when the mountain was still off-limits to Westerners.
- *A MOUNTAIN IN TIBET*, Charles Allen A history of British exploration of the Himalayas in the 19th Century, with a focus on Kailas
- *TRANS-HIMALAYA*, Sven Hedin (1970. $75.00. Greenwood.) The explorer's account of his 1907 expedition to Tibet, including his description of the first circumambulation of Kailas by a Westerner.
- *IN THE FORBIDDEN LAND*, A. H. Savage Landor A hair-raising tale of the author's illegal 1897 expedition to Mount Kailas. Hardship, bravado, torture, triumph—and some of it may even be true.
- *TREKKING IN TIBET*, Gary McCue (1991. $16.95. Mountaineers.) Detailed, expert, culturally sensitive. The best Tibet trekking guide.

Tibetan praying at a mani wall beside the Brahmaputra River (Tsangpo in Tibetan).

Llama-Trekking in Escalante Canyon

Is a llama merely a "glorified goat for yuppies and spaced-out New-Agers?" Or the best pack animal ever invented?

When President Clinton announced the creation of the 1.7 million acre Grand Staircase-Escalante National Monument in 1996, even the minority of wilderness-loving local residents had mixed feelings. Sure, it was great that the land was protected now, but the fear among some dedicated outdoorsmen and environmentalists was that a plague of tourists would soon infest the area. This National Monument thing, they realized, had blown the cover of the best-kept secret in the Southwest.

Not for a while yet. The handful of tourists now trickling into this remote corner of southern Utah mostly stay tethered to their cars, leaving a vast unspoiled wilderness of slickrock and twisting canyons for the rest of us to explore on foot. As that irascible Southwest guru Edward Abbey put it, "You can't see anything from a car; you've got to get out of the goddamned contraption and walk, better yet crawl, on hands and knees,

Late afternoon along the Escalante River, Grand Straircase-Escalante National Monument, southern Utah.

over the sandstone and through the thornbush and cactus. When traces of blood begin to mark your path, you'll see something, maybe."

Is there perhaps a middle ground, somewhere between automobiles and blood on the rocks? Enter Bevin and Steve Taylor, the proprietors of a literal mom-and-pop trekking outfitter called Red Rock 'n Llamas, in Boulder, Utah. Based in a self-constructed adobe-style dreamhouse at the end of a four-mile suspension-killing driveway up a red rock canyon, the Taylors run about a dozen 4-to-5-day treks each year in the Escalante, with llamas carrying the gear. These light-footed load-haulers make it possible to roam far out of dayhike range, deep into the heart of some of the most remote and surreal wilderness in the Lower 48, a labyrinth of wind- and water-sculpted slickrock and twisting canyons.

I was unprepared for the llama's appeal as a pack animal. This is primarily due to years of bitter anti-llama propaganda from my sister Becky, an old-fashioned Colorado mountain woman who for 20 years owned a lovable Mexican pack burro

named Jesus. The three of us spent many pleasant days walking the back country of Colorado and Utah, Jesus placidly and reliably carrying our food and camping gear. Beck, a traditionalist, contemptuously dismissed llamas as "glorified goats for yuppies and spaced-out New Agers."

Sorry, Beck. After five days trekking along the Upper Escalante River with Scout, Blue Moon, Drinian, and the rest of our four-footed pack crew, I am forced to concede that a llama is a very good pack animal indeed. They dutifully followed along behind us, with only an occasional tug of encouragement necessary on the lead rope. (Jesus, by contrast, would sometimes require emphatic carrot-and-stick encouragement from both ends simultaneously.) Much more agile and surefooted than a burro, the llamas easily hopped up and down waist-high riverbanks during our numerous stream crossings, and sloshed placidly along the river bottom itself for long stretches when the terrain so dictated. Because of their smaller loads—about 85 to 95 pounds each, compared to 120 to 150 pounds for a burro—light detachable packs can be carried, which speeds up

---

AT A GLANCE

TRIP LENGTH 7 days	PRICE RANGE (INDEPENDENT TREK)
TIME ON TREK 5 days	Not available
WALKING DISTANCE 35 miles	PRICE RANGE (OUTFITTED GROUP TREK)
MAXIMUM ALTITUDE 7,000 feet	$650–$1,000
PHYSICAL CHALLENGE ① 2 3 4 5	PRIME TIME July–August
MENTAL CHALLENGE 1 ② 3 4 5	STAGING CITY Boulder, Utah

the loading and unloading process considerably. Moreover, llamas are omnivorous eaters who can subsist entirely by foraging. Jesus, by contrast, required nightly oats to supplement his grazing.

Frustratingly, the llama's cute, cuddly appearance is belied by an aloof and independent nature. They don't like to be touched on their faces or heads. (Jesus, on the other hand, was

HIM TARZAN

A major source of entertainment on our trek was Matt Graham, a quiet, easygoing, longhaired, assistant guide who'd abandoned the life of a Huntington Beach surfer dude to become. . .well, Tarzan. Matt spent most of the trip barefoot and shirtless, to the delight of the female guests, who couldn't keep their eyes off his chiseled pecs and six-pack abs. Carrying his gear in a cloth sack slung over his shoulder, Matt would regularly stop to pick and eat various obscure desert plants, in the fashion of the Anasazi Indians who lived in these canyons a thousand years ago.

He has spent as long as six weeks out in the Escalante wilderness, alone, with nothing but a sack of rice and beans and the clothes on his back. (Hey, the guy lives in a teepee without electricity or running water, so it's not that big an adjustment.) Shoes? He makes his own sandals from vines and tire treads. Fire? When we challenged him to back up rumors that he could make fire from scratch, he disappeared into the bush for a few

minutes and returned with some bark, vines, sagebrush, tamarisk twigs, and a cow's ankle bone. While he fiddled expertly with this paraphernalia, a fellow trekker whispered, "This I gotta see. I learned all about making fire in Navy outdoor survival school, but not even our instructors could ever make it work in the real world." Three minutes later, a fire blazed.

Matt likes to run long distances, but considers marathons too short to be interesting. Instead, he prefers to, say, run the length of California along the Pacific Crest Trail (it took him 28 days). Or enter a 55-mile cross-country wilderness horse race—without the horse. Running in his homemade sandals, he led the field of 50-some four-legged equine competitors for the first 46 miles, but then made a wrong turn and eventually finished third, much to his disgust. Bewildered race officials gave him a bronze medal.

Matt Graham leads the llamas across the river.

On the high plateau, dotted with ponderosa pines.

more than happy to let Becky and I—along with virtually every passing backpacker—stroke his velvety muzzle or scratch his ears.) We did scratch the llamas' necks and pat their backs, but they couldn't have cared less whether we did or not. One woman on the trek reports, "Drinian seemed to like me, or so I thought at first. He kept blowing puffs of air into my ear (as I led him along), but what I thought was flirting turned out to be him exhaling as he nibbled plants. . . ."

Liberated from backpacking chores by the llamas, we were free to amble down the narrow canyon, gaze up at 600-foot high red rock walls, inspect Anasazi wall paintings and petroglyphs, ogle rock arches and natural bridges, and contemplate the vast Southwestern desert sky—all without seeing another human being in five days.

We swam in the river, or in natural swimming-pool size depressions in the sculptured slickrock where rainwater collected. One campsite was a huge red rock alcove reminiscent of the shell of the Hollywood Bowl, only much bigger. Another camp was set in front of a cave with the headroom and floorspace of a small house.

Campsites are chosen well away from streambeds due to the possibility of flash floods, which can be triggered by thunderstorms far upstream and out of earshot. On a Red Rock 'n Llamas trip here in 1998, trekkers were placidly crossing the Escalante in bright sunshine and ankle-deep water when the river suddenly turned muddy and began to rise. Within 15 seconds the water was waist-deep and the llamas were swimming. By holding hands the trekkers managed to

A narrow slot canyon with rock arches.

scramble safely ashore. Fortunately, the canyon was not particularly narrow at that point, and the group found a patch of high ground and watched the muddy torrent rise 15 feet in the next half hour. "Huge ponderosa pines were floating along smashing over the cottonwoods," recalls Steve Taylor. "You could hear boulders grinding and rumbling along the bottom as they were being swept downstream." During thunderstorm season—July and August—guides are always alert for sudden muddying of the river, and make sure that clients pass quickly through (or avoid altogether) narrow "slot canyons" that don't have immediate access to high ground. If worse came to worst, we were advised to float downstream feet first, with toes above the water to avoid entrapment in rocks or logs.

With the llamas shouldering the load, we were also freed from the tyranny of dehydrated backpacker food. Pancakes for breakfast, salmon sandwiches for lunch, chicken fajitas for dinner—we ate very well indeed. (On a previous trip, one of the guides, a marathon runner, was even dispatched back to the roadhead to bring in champagne and ice for a trekker's birthday.) River water was filtered before drinking—you never know what wild animals, not to mention the llamas, have been doing upstream—but we happily slurped from small springs flowing directly out of the rocks.

Despite its utter remoteness today, the Escalante has a long human history. The Anasazi, who inhabited much of the Southwest from about A.D. 200 until their abrupt and mysterious disappearance around the 13th century, built a few scattered cliff dwellings in Escalante Canyon. We saw a number of petroglyphs, wall paintings, and two ruins along our route. Six hundred years after the Anasazi came a handful of hardscrabble 19th-century Mormon settlers, who grazed their cattle

Opposite: Base camp beneath a long, thin waterfall.

THE SPITTIN' IMAGE

Reports of llama-spitting are in most cases wildly exaggerated. In five days in the company of nine llamas, I saw not a single incident of expectoration. "They mostly just spit at each other," says Bevin Taylor of Red Rock 'n Llamas, the outfitter for our trek. "The only thing you have to worry about is getting caught in a cross fire. And you always get plenty of warning. If you see them pull their ears back, raise their nose, and start wagging their tail, get out of the way." Llamas don't like being touched by humans on their faces and heads, and might spit in self-defense if so disturbed. But, assures Taylor, "If you don't provoke them, there's no problem at all."

Steve Taylor faces off with a llama.

and hacked a twisting wagon trail out of the rock through Escalante Canyon in order to haul a piano to the church in Boulder. We hiked along part of the road, barely discernible 100 years later. We made sure to leave no such traces for future Escalante wanderers.

THE ROUTE

From the not-yet-chic hamlet of Boulder, you'll drive in a hulking Chevy Suburban 25 miles down Highway 12 to the town of Escalante, passing through an extraordinary landscape of barren slickrock and twisting canyons. At the trailhead just outside the town of Escalante, you'll meet the llamas and follow a short trail to the Escalante River, a sandy, shallow, creek-sized stream that runs year-round. You'll head downstream along the canyon floor, walking sometimes along the sandy banks, sometimes in the riverbed itself. At a tributary stream, Mamie Creek, you'll turn up its side canyon, Death Hollow, to a camping spot under a huge natural red rock alcove.

The next day is a dayhike further up Death Hollow, with stops for swims and views of Anasazi petroglyphs before returning to the alcove camp. On Day 3 you'll pack up, descend Death Hollow back to the main Escalante, and continue downstream to a campsite near a cave just below a massive canyon wall called Imax. Day 4 is a dayhike up Sand Creek, a tributary just downstream from camp, to a beautiful rock pool along Willow Patch Creek. The return route to camp leads up out of the canyons and across a broad plain of undulating white slickrock. On Day 5 you'll pack up and proceed past cliff dwellings and the Escalante Natural Bridge to the trailhead along Highway 12, where the Suburban and llama trailer await for the drive back to Boulder.

WHAT TO EXPECT

This is a pleasant, low-key walk among some of the most surrealistic landscape on the planet. The pace is leisurely—six or seven miles a day—with mostly level walking along canyon floors. Much of the time you'll actually be sloshing along the streams themselves. (The water is rarely more than ankle-deep; take Tevas or an old pair of hiking boots you don't mind getting wet.) There's plenty of time for swimming (water temperature was a refreshing 70 to 75°F) and sightseeing along the way. The llamas add a great deal to the fun of the trip. If you want to, you may lead your own animal.

Surprisingly, we did not suffer from excessive heat. Even in July and August, the altitude (roughly 6,000 feet) was enough to take the edge off, and the route led mostly along canyon bottoms, often shaded by high rock walls and cottonwood trees. And there was water virtually always within a few steps. On our one major excursion up above the canyon rim, high clouds blocked the direct sun and kept temperatures manageable. Had there been no clouds, we would have stayed down in the canyons.

Although we were warned about scorpions, rattlesnakes, and poisonous cone-nosed kissing bugs, none made an appearance. The major visible hazards were the occasional thickets of poison ivy.

This is a great trek for feeling isolated. In five days, I saw no other people. You may see a few dayhikers near the beginning or end of the trek, or an occasional intrepid backpacker further in, but once well up into Death Hollow or Sand Creek, you'll be in a place no more than a few dozen people a year manage to find. With its modest pace, generally level terrain, and the cuddly llamas, it also a great family trek. According to the Taylors, kids as young as six or seven can manage the Upper Escalante trip.

GUIDES AND OUTFITTERS

It's easy to hike on your own in Escalante, but you'll be a backpacker, not a trekker. To take a trek as we've defined it—a long-distance multiday walk carrying only a light daypack—you'll need to use an outfitter to provide pack animals and the other usual trekking services. Red Rock 'n Llamas runs five or six trips a year along the

Upper Escalante, as well as three other itineraries in the Grand Staircase–Escalante National Monument. Escalante Canyon Outfitters, also located in Boulder, runs various treks in the Monument; they use packhorses to carry gear. If you insist on going independently, but still don't want to carry a heavy pack, Red Rock 'n Llamas will rent you a llama, provided you pass the mandatory half-day training session, for $45 a day plus drop-off and pick-up fees to the trailheads.

RED ROCK 'N LLAMAS
435-559-7325
www.gorp.com/redrock
$650–$750 for 4–5 days

ESCALANTE CANYON OUTFITTERS
888-326-4453
www.gorp.com/escalante
$695–$990 for 4–6 days

RECOMMENDED READING

■ *DESERT SOLITAIRE*, Edward Abbey (1990. $12.00. Simon & Schuster.) A series of essays by the beloved chronicler of the American Southwest about his stint as a ranger in Arches National Park in the 1960s, when virtually nobody went there.

■ *CANYONEERING 3: LOOP HIKES IN UTAH'S ESCALANTE*, Steve Allen (1997. $21.95. University of Utah Press.) The best current hiking guidebook to the Escalante area, written by a local resident who's been exploring the area for decades.

■ *HIKING THE ESCALANTE*, Rudi Lebreski Now out of print, this is the guide recommended by Bevin and Steve Taylor of Red Rock 'n Llamas.

The Darien Gap

*" . . . less a piece of terrain than a state of mind,
a wild frontier utterly divorced from the moral inhibitions
of normal human society."*

The Pan American Highway is billed as the world's longest road, a 19,000-mile asphalt and gravel ribbon that stretches from Tierra del Fuego to Alaska. But there is a 230-mile missing link in the famed highway, where the jungle and terrain have defeated the best efforts of 20th-century (and so far, even 21st-century) roadbuilders and their D9 Caterpillars. The Darien Gap, a 3.7-million acre coast-to-coast swath of roadless jungle astride the narrow isthmus of southern Panama, stands as a last defiant stretch of wilderness separating North and South America.

The first Darien Gap trekker was Vasco Nunez de Balboa, the Spanish explorer who discovered the Pacific Ocean in 1513. (Of course the entire hemisphere was a gap in those days.) A settler in the Spanish colony of Hispaniola (now Cuba), Balboa skipped out on his clamoring creditors and stowed away on a supply ship that even-

Pavarando, the last Embera village on the Rio Sambu, on the edge of the mountains.

tually landed on what is now the southern coast of Panama. The ship's crew established the colony of Darien, where the charismatic Balboa became the unofficial governor. During expeditions into the jungle, Indians told him tales of a great sea across the mountains. Hoping to pull off some spectacular feat to gain the notice of King Ferdinand (and hopefully be named the official governor), Balboa set off in September 1513 to find the great ocean, with about 90 compatriots and an army of Indian guides and porters.

After three weeks of arduous trekking through the jungle, his Indian guides told him he would be able to see the sea from a nearby mountain. Balboa hiked alone to the summit and became the first European to see the Pacific.

Sadly, his feat did not bring him the anticipated glory—quite the contrary, in fact. Before news of Balboa's discovery reached the King, Ferdinand had appointed another governor of Darien, an insecure and jealous fellow who correctly saw Balboa as a potential rival for the king's favors. The governor trumped up some phony charges and had Balboa arrested for treason, convicted in a kangaroo court, and beheaded.

Little has changed in the Darien in the ensuing half-millenium. Although we now call it a rain forest instead of a jungle, the Darien remains one of the world's most inhospitable, unexplored, and biologically diverse places. It is home to 7,000 plant species, 1,500 varieties of trees, and 800 birds. The region's astonishing biodiversity has made it a magnet for biologists.

Wade Davis, author and Harvard-trained ethnobotanist, has spent much of his life wandering Latin American rain forests. A decade before the first trekker set foot in the place, he and an eccentric English companion bridged the Darien Gap on foot, from the Colombian border to the town of Santa Fe—in the height of the rainy season, no less. His description of the place gives trekkers a tantalizing—if somewhat foreboding—preview.

"We entered a world of plants, water, and silence," writes Davis. "We moved from one Embera or Kuna village to the next, soliciting new guides and obtaining provisions as we went along . . .each day we became part of a veil that gradually enveloped us as the forest closed in, absorbing our party as the ocean swallows a diver.

AT A GLANCE

TRIP LENGTH 14 days	PRICE RANGE (INDEPENDENT TREK)
TIME ON TREK 10 days	Not recommended
WALKING DISTANCE 65 miles	PRICE RANGE (OUTFITTED GROUP TREK) $2,495
MAXIMUM ALTITUDE 1,150 feet	PRIME TIME January–March
PHYSICAL CHALLENGE 1 2 ③ 4 5	STAGING CITY Panama City, Panama
MENTAL CHALLENGE 1 2 3 ④ 5	

TRAVELS WITH CHARLIE

Is there something about the jungle, some implacable *Heart of Darkness* thing, that brings out the weirdness in people? "For some reason, this trek seems to attract a lot of loose cannons," says Andrew Gilchrist of Lost World Adventures, the trek outfitter.

Consider Charlie from Brooklyn, who participated in the first Darien Gap trek in 1993. A fellow trekker, adventure writer Larry Rice, tells the tale:

"As usual, last in line was Charlie, the grey-haired 50-year-old shipping and receiving clerk from Brooklyn . . . .Charlie was a throwback to the beatnik era. He played bongos and even said 'Daddy-O.' He wore black pull-on motorcycle boots with big brass buckles across the instep, a huge straw hat, and blue jeans that were heavy and hot and never dried out. . .Charlie kept falling farther and farther behind because he kept stopping to drain the water from his motorcycle boots Finally, an irritated Hernan (the head guide) gave him an ultimatum: 'Either you cut holes in your boots right now for drainage, or I will shoot holes in your boots, with your feet still in them.'

"All Charlie wanted to do was sleep and fuss about personal hygiene. . .awake from his nap and busily flossing his teeth, (he) griped that we weren't getting enough to eat. . . .A professed nudist, Charlie admitted that one of the main reasons he joined the expedition was the lure of encountering Darien Indian women living au naturel. One of the first things Charlie asked Hernan upon meeting him was if it was possible to buy X-rated videos of Choco Indians in Panama City. . . .To add to his list of culturally insensitive activities, Charlie went around propositioning native women in one of the villages we visited. . .the men in the village didn't take kindly to Charlie's overtures. . .(we) almost (got) into a war with the Indians. . . .(We tried to) tell Charlie to stop acting like a jerk. . . .He was impervious to peer pressure. We yelled, mocked, cajoled, threatened, even explained, but all to no avail. He just didn't get it."

"It was during those days that I first experienced the overwhelming grandeur of the tropical forest. It is a subtle thing. There are no herds of ungulates, as on the Serengeti Plain, no cascades of orchids—just a thousand shades of green, an infinitude of shape, form, and texture. . . .It is almost as if you have to close your eyes to behold the constant hum of biological activity—evolution, if you will—working in overdrive. . . .There are no flowers, at least few that can be readily seen, and with the blazing sun hovering motionless at midday there are few sounds. In the air there is a fluid heaviness, a weight of centuries, of years without seasons, of life without rebirth. One can walk for hours and remain convinced that not a mile has been gained.

"Then toward dusk everything changes. The air cools, the light becomes amber, and the open sky above the swamps and rivers fills with darting swallows and swifts, kiskadees and flycatchers. The hawks, herons, jacanas, and kingfishers of the river margins give way to flights of cackling parrots, sun-grebes, and nunbirds, and spectacular displays of toucans and scarlet macaws. Squirrel monkeys appear, and from the riverbanks emerge caiman, eyes poking out of the water, tails and bodies still and dull as driftwood. In the light of dusk one can finally discern shapes in the forest—sloths clinging to the limbs of cecropia trees, vipers entwined in branches, tapir wallowing in distant sloughs. For a brief moment at twilight the forest seems of a human scale and somehow

"Then toward dusk. . .the air cools, the light becomes amber, and the open sky above the. . .rivers fills with darting swallows and swifts...."

TREKKING

Top: Red-lored Amazon parrot.
Above: Village, Playa del Muerto, in the Darien jungle

lost, or, at best, only vaguely aware of where we were. Free of distractions, one became honed by life in the forest. . . .I noted the simple luxuries of forest life; the smoke of a fire that chases away the insects, a rainless night, a thatch hut found in the woods, a banana almost gone bad lying in a trough, abandoned plantings of manioc, a fresh kill, . . .water deep enough to bathe in, a hint of a solid shit, a full night's sleep. . .

"After just a fortnight on the trail, our passage began to take on the tone of a dream. In part this was because we rarely slept. With the rain sleep was not often possible. At the end of long days we simply lay in our hammocks in an unnatural rest, like a state of trance, dulled by exhaustion and insulated from the night by mosquito netting and the smoke of a smoldering fire. But mostly we became infected by the spirit of the place. The Darien turned out to be less a piece of terrain than a state of mind, a wild frontier utterly divorced from the moral inhibitions of normal human society."

THE ROUTE

The Trans-Darien trek roughly approximates the ocean-to-ocean route of Balboa when he discovered the Pacific in 1519. Trekkers fly into Panama City, then take a charter flight to Puerto Obaldia. After a quick side trip by dugout canoe, or "bongo," to La Miel, the last Panamanian village before the Colombian border, you'll hike up a 1,000-foot cliff to the Kuna Indian Village of Armilla. From there, you'll hike and walk through Kuna coconut plantations along the coast to a camp set at the mouth of the Pito River. There you'll enter the rain forest and cross the Continental Divide to a camp at the headwaters of the Membrillo River. The trail follows the Membrillo for four days, to its confluence with the Chucunaque, at which point you'll board dugout canoes for the day-long run to El Real de Santa Maria, an Afro-darienite town on the Tuira River, and

manageable. But then with the night comes the rain and later the sounds of insects running wild through the trees until, with the dawn, once again silence. The air becomes still and the steam rises from the cool earth. White fog lies all about like something solid, all-consuming."

At one point, Davis recounts how the party's Kuna guides lost their bearings. ". . .for the next week we wandered through the forest

Boys in the village of Pavarando try to hit birds with slingshots.

thence downriver to the Pacific port town of La Palma. From there it's a short flight back to Panama City.

WHAT TO EXPECT

This trek could be your worst jungle nightmare. Oppressive heat and humidity, snakes, bugs, and the possibility of malaria, blisters, and jungle rot in various extremities are all part of the package. You'll spend many hours sloshing through swampy areas and along shallow rivers, and your socks will almost certainly be wet for the entire trip. After some early clients showed up wearing motorcycle boots and deck shoes, the outfitter now requires clients to wear special military-style jungle boots, with drainage holes. (They even provide a brand name and model number

to order, from a military boot supplier located in—get this—Darien, Georgia.) Even these special boots may not assure comfortable feet; the outfitter's equipment list also includes a "blister kit" and labels this particular item "Important!" Get the hint?

But it's not all misery. The swimming is good in the occasional clear jungle pool. And there even looms the possibility of great riches—some of the riverbeds you'll travel contain flakes of gold, and trekkers will have the opportunity to do a bit of panning.

The trek features plenty of interaction with the local people, who rarely see outsiders and don't generally cater to them—although the Kuna tribesmen in the village of Armilla will be happy to sell you some *molas*, their

Ardino Caisamo, village chief of Condoto, poles his dugout up Rio Venado.

GUIDES AND OUTFITTERS

This trek should be done with a guide or group. The route passes through three autonomous regions where the local people make their own laws and take a dim view of outsiders who show up unannounced. "At best, they'd kick you out, at worst it could be dangerous," says Andrew Gilchrist of Lost World Adventures, the trip's American outfitter. On the first trans-Darien trip, suspicious Kuna villagers confiscated trekkers' gear for three days until they could confirm that permission had indeed been granted by tribal leaders. Other Kuna villages have been known to charge hikers $40 each just to pass through. The Darien Gap itself—the vague 125-mile network of foot trails that connect the Colombian and Panamanian ends of the Pan American highway—is a favorite route of Colombian guerrillas, drug smugglers, and bandits.

Lost World works in conjunction with Ancon Expeditions, the Panamanian company that actually operates the trip. Ancon's president is currently the mayor of Panama City, and its chief guide, Hernan Arauz, pioneered the trek back in 1993 and has worked since then to maintain good relations with the indigenous people along the route. Essentially, if you want to trek across the Darien, you go with Hernan. Trekkers wishing to do the route independently should contact Ancon (011-507-269-9414; fax 264-3713; www.ecopanama.com) and try to work something out.

Independent trekking in other parts of the Darien is possible, although difficult and somewhat risky. About 100 gringos a year actually trek the Gap itself, starting at the end of a dirt extension of the Pan American highway in Yaviza and proceeding up the Tuira Valley by foot and boat to the Indian villages of Pucuro and Paya and on into Colombia. But beware of drug runners, illegal immigrants, and other unsavory types who will be sharing the trail with you.

In addition to the trans-Darien route, Lost

traditional decorative cloths. You'll also get to know your camp staff. Each trekker is assigned his own personal porter/guide to carry loads, set up tents, share his vast knowledge of the forest and its creatures, and generally keep an eye on you.

World also offers an easier trek itinerary in the Darien that focuses more on culture and wildlife and less on coast-to-coast territorial conquest.

LOST WORLD ADVENTURES
800-999-0558
www.lostworldadventures.com
$2,495 for 14 days

RECOMMENDED READING

■ *THROUGH THE DARIEN GAP: AN ADVENTURER'S GUIDE*, Patricia Upton A 40-page photocopied self-published guide by an adventurous couple who have crossed the Gap five times. The emphasis is on travel by dirt-bike or off-road vehicle, but there is some advice on walking and some interesting anecdotes about the Darien area. (Available from Adventurous Traveler.com)

■ *BACKPACKING IN CENTRAL AMERICA*, Burford (1996. $15.95. Bradt Publications.) A section on Darien with some useful tips for general hiking and backpacking.

■ *THE PATH BETWEEN THE SEAS*, David McCulloch (1999. $18.00. Simon & Schuster.) Not directly relevant to Darien trekking, but anyone who walks across Panama from Atlantic to Pacific should read this classic account of the construction of the Panama Canal.

Ferns at the edge of the cloud forest.

Foothills of the Tian Shan

"It seems incredible that such wide reaches of the noblest kind of land should be so scantly held."

In 1926, American adventurer Owen Lattimore set off on a two-year trip by horseback through the remote mountains and deserts of central Asia. Near the end of his epic journey, Lattimore rode into the Tekes Valley in the northern foothills of the Tian Shan Mountains, a range of icebound peaks that stretches 1,500 miles across what are today the former Soviet republics of Kazakhstan and Kyrgyzstan, and the Chinese frontier province of Xinjiang. "Riding through the magnificent valley of the Tekes," Lattimore wrote, "past endless alps of high pasture and lordly forests, the traveler wonders at the scantiness of population. It seems incredible that such wide reaches of the noblest kind of land should be so scantly held."

Seventy-three years later, our small group of adventurers was trekking through the high pastures and still-lordly forests of the Tekes Valley in southeastern Kazakhstan. We too noted the scant-

"The feel of this trek is more like Colorado than Nepal—beautiful big green valleys strewn with woods, meadows, and lakes...."

KAZAKHSTAN

Lake
Balkash

Almaty Tekes
Valley

TIAN SHAN

KYRGYZSTAN

CHINA

iness of population, but with more foreboding than wonder. For we were badly lost, separated from our Kazakh guide—the only one of us who knew the way—and unable to find our camp as a windswept rain began to fall and the sun settled over the low, grassy hills and the steppes beyond.

Eventually we spotted a yurt—the traditional felt-covered portable dwelling of the nomadic herders who roam these valleys in summer—along the riverbank, a thin column of smoke rising from its stovepipe chimney. As we approached, the nomad family, which had already assembled outside to view the passing of the peculiar visitors, smiled shyly and quickly offered us refuge from the rain. Squatting on Oriental rugs next to a woodstove, we made small talk through our Russian-speaking trip leader, ate homemade cheese and bread, and sipped bowls of *kumys*, the tangy buzz-inducing fermented mare's milk that has been the staple of Asian nomads for centuries. "Do you get many Americans up this way?" we asked our hosts. "You're the first," came the answer.

It's quite possible that we were indeed the first Americans to set foot in the Tekes Valley—or any of the other nearby valleys of the northern Tian Shan—since Lattimore. Stalin closed off this area of Kazakhstan near the Chinese border in the 1930s, and it remained forbidden to foreigners until the breakup of the Soviet Union in 1989. Since then, a handful of Western climbers have helicoptered into the nearby Central Tian Shan to climb peaks like 22,949-foot Khan Tengri and 24,405-foot Peak Pobeda, but for trekkers this was terra incognita.

Not for long. "Without a doubt, Soviet Central Asia is the next great trekking area," predicts Rob Smurr, a Ph.D. candidate in Russian history, trekking guide for Mountain Travel-Sobek, and the leader of our exploratory trek. "People have been trekking in the Himalayas and the Andes for 30 years now, and they're looking for something new and exotic. Central Asia is the

Overleaf: Khan Tengri (22,949 feet), in the Central Tian Shan, during a 1991 winter attempt, the first ever.

AT A GLANCE

TRIP LENGTH 16 days
TIME ON TREK 10 days
WALKING DISTANCE 90–100 miles
MAXIMUM ALTITUDE 12,400 feet
PHYSICAL CHALLENGE 1 ② 3 4 5
MENTAL CHALLENGE 1 ② 3 4 5

PRICE RANGE (INDEPENDENT TREK) Impractical (see page 171)
PRICE RANGE (OUTFITTED GROUP TREK) $2,950–$3,450 (depends on group size)
PRIME TIME July–August
STAGING CITY Almaty, Kazakhstan
HEADS UP Trekking here is in its infancy; expect the unexpected.

obvious next step."

Soviet Central Asia—historically known as Turkestan and today consisting of the newly independent re-publics of Kyrgyzstan, Tajikistan, Turkmenistan, Uzbekistan, and the southeastern part of Kazahkstan—has a number of attractions for the trekker. First, of course, there's the scenery: the broad valleys of pine forests, flower-strewn meadows, Yosemite-like rock faces, and snow-covered 24,000-foot peaks of the Tian Shan and Pamir Mountains. And when we gazed from several high passes at the main peaks of the central Tian Shan, perhaps 15 miles away, the vista was Himalayan in its sweep.

"OWEN LATTIMORE AND THE faithful Moses, 1926," from Lattimore's High Tartary, *a narrative of his epic two-year journey by horseback across central Asia, including the Tekes Valley.*

But it takes more than scenery to make a great trek. For me, our rescue by the hospitable nomads—and a second visit with another family that turned into an hour-long gabfest—were high points of the trip. "The people you meet along the trail haven't been spoiled yet by Western values," says Smurr. "Hospitality to passersby is an integral part of nomad culture." Even the prosaic practicalities of the region favor the trekker; because the local mountain people have de-pended on horses for thousands of years, beasts of burden are easily available to schlepp camping gear. (The idea of human porters, à la Nepal, is laughable to the Kazakhs, who consider their horses as indispensable as Americans do their cars.) Although our horses and horsemen seemed unaccus-tomed to dealing with large loads—the first morning's packing-up resembled a rodeo at times—they quickly got the hang of it.

It is the nature of exploratory treks to be screwed up—somebody's got to go first and make all the mistakes—and ours held true to form even before we laced up our hiking boots. For starters,

DARKER HUMOR

Kazakhstan's population is only about half ethnic Kazakhs, descended from the traditional nomads native to the area. More than a third of Kazakh citizens are eth-nic Russians, the legacy of Russia's century-long domi-nation of the area. Although the political balance of power has shifted since Kazakh independence in 1991, Russians still dominate Kazakhstan economically and culturally, with Russian being the primary language of the cities and towns. Our trek staff reflected the ethnic divisions of the country; the horsemen who took care of our packhorses lived in the mountains and were Kazakhs, while our three guides and cook were Russians who lived in Almaty.

Sitting around the campfire one night, roasting apples and listening to the guides, we got a sample of the cynical, self-loathing Russian sense of humor. Valeri hardly cracked a smile as he related the following joke: Russian guy finds a magic lamp. The genie says "I'll grant you one wish, but whatever I give you, your neighbor gets double." Russian guy thinks a minute and says, "Okay, gouge out one of my eyes."

the former Soviet Army GAZ-66 all-terrain troop carrier truck we were riding across the steppe to our first camp lost its brakes on a hill, rolled down backwards, and flipped over. (Amazingly, no one was seriously injured.) Next, walking on to camp without our Kazakh guide Valeri—he'd borrowed a horse and ridden ahead to bring back packhorses to retrieve our luggage from the wreck—we began the feckless trudge that eventually led to our fortuitous nomad encounter. (We subsequently got our bearings and stumbled into camp just before dark.) Finally, Valeri fell off his horse crossing the river to camp and apparently broke a rib. Were we having fun yet?

Well, yes. We spent the next ten days treading faint trails along steep, wildflower-carpeted meadows, ascending rubble-strewn glacial cirques, and struggling up and over 12,000-foot passes of soft, boot-sucking scree, and gazing out at the icy white horizon-to-horizon wall of the central Tian Shan. Our trekking route evoked at various times Colorado's South San Juan Mountains, Switzerland's Engadine Valley, and Wyoming's Wind River Range. Among this noblest kind of landscape, we saw no other people for eight days.

The trek's exclamation point was a terrifying scenic flight among the high peaks of the Central Tian Shan in a former Soviet Army Mi-8 troop carrier helicopter. (Pay no attention to that man behind the cowling banging on the engine with a hammer just before takeoff, nor the cargo of leaking propane cylinders under your feet, nor the utter lack of seat belts—or for that matter, seats.) On the approach to Khan Tengri, the chopper flew up a valley two or three ridges over from our trekking route. Gazing out the window, Smurr said to no one in particular, "Man, this is the most beautiful valley I've ever seen. We gotta come here next year and check it out on the ground." In Central Asia, it seems, there's always someplace new to explore.

Top: Peaceful meals in side valleys of the Tekes were offset by the Soviet Army troop carrier's brake failure and subsequent roll-over on a hill. No one was seriously injured.

THE ROUTE

You'll fly into Almaty (formerly known as Alma-Ata), a modern Soviet-built city of 1.3 million people, saved from terminal drabness only by the profusion of trees that line virtually every street. Only a wooden Orthodox church and an

old hunting lodge converted to a museum of musical instruments are of architectural note.

After a day in Almaty to recover from jet lag and see the few sights, you'll take a bus east across the steppe for six hours to a highway checkpoint, where a GAZ-66 all-terrain troop carrier takes over for the two-hour grind along a rough dirt track to the first camping spot on the banks of the Tekes River. (Hopefully, the truck's brakes will work this time). You'll then trek up the Tekes Valley for three days, virtually to its source, before crossing a steep scree pass with views of the main peaks of the Tian Shan from about 12,000 feet. The route then leads into the high reaches of the Tuyuk-Kokpak valley, where you'll camp for two nights. During the layover day, you'll have the option to hang out at camp, climb to the top of a nearby ridge with more great views of the big peaks, or take a walk with crampons along a high glacier. You'll then cross two more high passes and trek by a couple of high-altitude lakes before descending to a final camp near the military border outpost at Bayankol. From here you can take the optional two-hour helicopter sightseeing trip into the heart of the central Tian Shan, with brief stopovers at two climbers' base camps. (At $100, this flight may be the world's best bargain in thrill rides.) From Bayankol you'll bus back to Almaty.

Note that this itinerary is subject to change. Lessons learned from the exploratory will be applied to future trips, and that magical valley on the way to Khan Tengri still beckons.

WHAT TO EXPECT

The feel of this trek is more like Colorado than Nepal—beautiful big green valleys strewn with woods, meadows, and lakes, with some nice little rocky peaks usually in view and a glacier peeking over the ridge here and there. Although the giant 20,000-footers of the Central Tian

THE FAMILY PORTRAIT taken by the author (above) bears an amazing resemblance to that taken in 1927 by Owen Lattimore (top) of a Kazakh family group. The similarities held up, right down to the nomads' simple yurt dwelling and shy yet hospitable greeting to strangers.

Shan are no more than 15 or 20 miles away from where you'll be trekking, you'll see them only occasionally, when crossing high passes or on the optional glacier walk along a high ridge. Even then, don't expect a close-up presence à la the Himalayas. (For that, there's the helicopter flight, more akin to an IMAX movie than a real-life experience.) If you seek a Himalayan-style walk among looming snowcapped giants, this is not the trek.

The physical demands are modest by Himalayan standards. With the exception of three

The giant 20,000-footers of the Central Tian Shan are no more than 15 to 20 miles away from the route.

The mountain people still depend on horses, so that beasts of burden are easily available to carry camping gear.

steep passes, the climb gradients are mostly gradual. The pass crossings, however, can be quite steep, with switchbacks twisting up long scree slopes. Altitude, which typically ranges from 9,000 to 11,000 feet, is high enough to induce extra huffing and puffing, but altitude sickness should not be a problem. (Still, be sure to drink lots of water.)

The trails, usually used by horses instead of walkers, are generally good at lower altitudes, but in some of the high pastures they become faint and difficult to follow. (Feel free to bushwhack; since you're usually walking along broad, open valleys, it's hard to get lost.) The footing can be difficult in places, particularly descending the passes, which tend to be either loose scree or slick grass.

At the lower elevations you'll meet nomads who will probably invite you in for *kumys*, lost or not. But the higher pastures have been closed to grazing in recent years, so for most of the trip you'll be isolated from other people. (The chance of meeting other trekkers is virtually zero.) This isolation is perhaps the greatest danger of the trip; in case of illness or injury, help is very far away. Evacuation by horseback is the most likely scenario, but it may be possible to contact the helicopter at nearby Kahn Tengri base camp in a dire emergency. Radio communication is dicey, requiring a guide to climb to the top of a ridge, string up an antenna, and hope for the best.

The weather is generally good, with blue skies and temperatures touching 80°F in the day and about 50 at night. Rain is possible, however. Before we arrived, it had been raining nonstop for a week, and we got wet on several occasions.

Food on our trek was excellent, thanks to the talents of our young ethnic Russian cook, Nikolai. Somehow, he made mashed potatoes and sausage for breakfast not only bearable but pleasurable, and his spaghetti sauce, prepared with an herb he picked along the way (whose identity he declined to reveal), was the best I have ever eaten by a factor of three or four.

GUIDES AND OUTFITTERS

On-your-own trekking in this area is impractical. There are no hiking or trekking maps as such, and the topo maps of the area are too large in scale to be really useful. Because trekking has never been done here, there is no local network of guides. Only a handful of local shepherds know this country well, and none of them speak English, of course—although you might be able to communicate in Russian. Practically speaking, your only choice for our particular itinerary is Mountain Travel-Sobek, the U.S. outfitter that ran our trek.

LOCAL OUTFITTERS

Asia Tourism in Almaty provides guides, packhorses, and local transportation for Mountain Travel. The Kazakh firm was founded in 1991 by mountaineer Renat Khaibullin, and operates the two climbers' base camps at Khan Tengri. It also offers various tours, treks, and climbs in other parts of the Tian Shan. Asia Tourism's 1999-2000 catalog lists a trip similar to Mountain Travel's at the astonishingly low price of $790, but in fact the company has never operated the trek on its own, only as a subcontractor for Mountain Travel. Other local trekking operators include Tien Shan Travel in Bishkek, Kyrgyzstan. (011-3312-270576).

ASIA TOURISM
011-3272-631-227
www.asiatour.org

U.S. OUTFITTERS
MOUNTAIN TRAVEL-SOBEK
888-687-6235
www.mtsobek.com
$2,950–$3,450 for 16 days

A number of other outfitters run treks in Central Asia, although not the specific routes listed here. They include REI Adventures (800-622-2236); and KE Adventure Travel (800-497-9675).

RECOMMENDED READING

■ *TREKKING IN RUSSIA AND CENTRAL ASIA,* Frith Maier (1994. $16.95. Mountaineers.) Although it doesn't describe the specific area of this trek, this is the most authoritative source on trekking in Central Asia.

■ *LONELY PLANET GUIDE TO CENTRAL ASIA,* Andrew Humphries et al Best general guide for exploring and/or finding accommodations in the cities and towns. No hard-core trekking info, however.

■ *HIGH TARTARY,* Owen Lattimore (1994. $15.00. Kodansha.) A narrative of Lattimore's 1926 to 1927 journey by horseback through central Asia with his wife, including the Tekes Valley—although Lattimore rode downstream from our trek route, just across the Chinese border.

■ *TURKISTAN: NOTES OF A JOURNEY IN RUSSIAN TURKISTAN, KHOKAND, BUKHARA AND KULDJA,* Eugene Schuyler (1999. $125.00. Reprint Services Corp.) Published 1876. Lots of info about local people and customs.

Copper Canyon

The "Grand Canyon of Mexico" has cave-dwelling
Indian footracers who can run your sorry butt into the ground.

I t's almost impossible to read an outfitter's brochure about Copper Canyon, 300 miles south of the border in the midst of the Sierra Madre mountains, without encountering the phrase "four times bigger than the Grand Canyon." Technically, that's true. But because Copper Canyon is a broad complex of six canyons, there's no one place you can stand and get that famous jaw-dropping view of overwhelming immensity.

So Copper Canyon is *not* the Grand Canyon, or anything like it. But that's all right. Come to think of it, that's good. Instead of arid red rock, there is a profusion of plant life—100 species of oak and pine trees along the rim; bougainvillea, hibiscus, bamboo, fig, and mango trees on the canyon floor. Instead of rattlesnakes and scorpions (okay, in addition to rattlesnakes and scorpions) there are butterflies and russet-crowned motmots, macaws, parrots, and hummingbirds. And instead of long-abandoned remnants of Anasazi cliff

Consulting a map to find the way through the canyons of the Sierra Madre.

dwellings, Copper Canyon harbors natural caves inhabited by real live Tara-humara Indians.

The first Tarahumara cave I saw triggered wildly contrasting emotions. The first was sympathy for a people apparently so primitive as to be literal cavemen. The second, which followed a millisecond later, was, my God, what a glorious place to live; a cavernous loft with built-in A/C, southern exposure, and a view that Donald Trump would pay $10 million for—if he could buy it. But he can't.

Don't worry about the Tarahumara. They certainly don't pay much attention to us. A shy, innocent, and cheerful people isolated from modern civilization by virtually impassable terrain, they come closer than any other North American culture to the ideal of the "noble savage" living in splendid isolation from the ills of modern society.

Four hundred years ago, the Tarahumara roamed throughout the Sierra Madre. But in the 1600s, Jesuit missionaries bent on "civilizing" the natives drove them off their land and essentially enslaved them. After 50 years of futile resistance—culminating in 1697 when a Spanish commander killed 30 rebellious Tarahumara, decapitated them, and mounted their heads on spears along a main road—the Tarahumara changed their tactics to evasion and retreat, and began moving into remote canyons, out of reach of their "saviors." It was a tactic that ultimately proved successful; the Tarahumara are still there, living pretty much the way they always have.

The Tarahumara are famed for their prowess in long-distance running. (Their own name for their tribe is Raramuri, or "fast runners.") They never really developed hunting implements—spears, bows and arrows—because the Tarahumara method of hunting is to simply run after an animal until it drops from exhaustion. A Tarahumara supposedly once ran 600 miles in five days to deliver an important message. (By contrast, Pheidippides, the Greek soldier who ran from Marathon to Athens with news of victory over the Persians—and then dropped dead—covered a piddling 26 miles.)

Traditional races, called *rarajipari*, pit teams of runners from one village against another over distances of up to 150 miles. (The modern Tarahumara must be going soft; a recent race between the villagers of Yerba Buena and

AT A GLANCE

TRIP LENGTH 8–10 days	**PRICE RANGE (INDEPENDENT TREK)** $150–$300
TIME ON TREK 4–6 days	**PRICE RANGE (OUTFITTED GROUP TREK)**
WALKING DISTANCE 26–28 miles	$1,100–$1,400
MAXIMUM ALTITUDE 6,500 feet	**PRIME TIME** November–February
PHYSICAL CHALLENGE 1 ②　3　4　5	**STAGING CITY** Chihuahua, Mexico
MENTAL CHALLENGE 1 ②　3　4　5	

Top: In Copper Canyon vertical gains—and losses—of 5,000 feet a day are possible. Above: 400 years ago Jesuit missionaries tried to convert the cave-dwelling Tarahumara Indians.

Coyachique covered a mere 60 miles—20 laps of a three-mile loop.) The criterium-style format is preferred so that villagers—drinking, cheering, the women dressed in their finest clothes—can follow the progress of the race and the prospects for the huge wagers that typically ride on the outcome.

Each team of runners has its own medicine man, who conjures up potions to help the runners and to cast bad luck on the opposing team. Ground-up human bones are sometimes buried secretly along the trail to rob opposing runners of their strength. Before the races, runners ritualistically drink *tesguino*, an alcohol made of corn, and smoke a combination of tobacco and dried bats' blood to help them run faster and repel the other team's evil spells.

Perhaps because running comes so easily to the Tarahumara, they add a wrinkle to the *rarajapari* to make it even more challenging: Each team must kick a small wooden ball for the entire race. The winner is the first team to get the ball across the line. Accomplished kickers can boot the ball up to 100 yards with astonishing accuracy. Kicking duty rotates from man to man while other team members rush ahead to locate the ball and minimize the search time for an errant kick.

Tarahumaras have raced against elite distance runners on several occasions. In the 1928 Olympic marathon, a pair of Tarahumaras finished a scant three minutes behind the winner. Apparently unaware of the distance of the 26-mile race, they crossed the finish line barely winded and incredulous that the race was over so soon, shouting "Too short! Too short!"

In 1992 a contingent of five Tarahumara runners was brought north by an American, Rick Fisher, and entered in the Leadville 100, a grueling 100-mile wilderness trail run through the mountains of Colorado that many consider the world's most difficult footrace, if not its most difficult athletic competition. Unfamiliar with the ways of the white man, the Tarahumara were too shy to take the food and water at the runners' aid stations along the course. (They didn't realize it was meant for them, too.) Given flashlights for the night segments of the race, they pointed them straight up, like the torches they used back home during their village races. Dehydrated and starved for glycogen, they dropped out after 30 miles.

But in 1993, they tried again. This time, the Tarahumara runners took food and water at the aid stations, and pointed their flashlights at the ground. They even wore fancy new running shoes

Copper Canyon is lush, home to 100 species of oak, bougainvillea, hibiscus, fig, and mango trees, as well as macaws, parrots, hummingbirds, and russet-crowned motmots.

in place of their usual tire-tread sandals, called huaraches. (Not that they went totally native; the Indian runners dutifully took their customary pre-race nips of *tesguino* and got in a couple of ritual smokes.) After 13 miles, the lead group of three Tarahumaras threw away their shoes and donned their trusty huaraches. Twenty hours later, the trio of Tarahumara crossed the finish line first, second, and fifth, soundly defeating the world's best ultramarathon racers, fewer than half of whom even finished. The winner, Victoriano Churro, was 55 years old. Finally, the Tarahumara had found a race that wasn't too short.

THE ROUTE

From Chihuahua, you'll take the renowned Copper Canyon train (or a bus) to Creel, a small logging village on a plateau above the canyon. From there it's a hair-raising jeep ride down a twisting dirt road to Batopilas, an old silver mining town at the bottom of the canyon that still has a few relics of bygone Victorian splendor. The most popular trekking route is the four- or five-day up-and-down hike to Urique, another river town in the next drainage over. There are various routes; the most popular runs along the old aqueduct to Las Juntas, the village of Cerro Colorado, over Mesa Yerbanis, down into Urique Canyon and on to Urique. Trekkers then drive out of the canyon and meet the train back to Chihuahua.

WHAT TO EXPECT

Although Copper Canyon has certain similarities to Nepal—a beautiful, rugged, roadless landscape

EXPERIENCE TOTAL RELEASE

To get a feel for the primitive nature of Copper Canyon trekking, one has only to scan the release and waiver of liability signed by all members of the Canyon Crossing Expedition operated by Copper Canyon Hiking Lodges. Refreshingly free of legal mumbo-jumbo, the waiver reads as follows:

"I understand that the Canyon Crossing Expedition in which I am participating is inherently dangerous. It is additionally dangerous because we will be traveling largely like the Tarahumara do. There is no way to escape easily to civilization in case of injury. No doctor or medical facilities are available. No radio. No satellite locator, rescue beacon, no one trained in first aid or CPR. . . . There are poisonous snakes, insects, scorpions, vampire bats, possibility of landslides, lightning, falls, hail, dangerous river crossings, drug plantations. . . . I understand that experienced guides have stated this trip is too difficult and dangerous for non-professionals. There is no possibility of helicopter evacuation.

"I understand there is no guarantee of success. The river may be too high, landslides may block the trail, or injuries may require us to turn back. Sometimes we mis-calculate the food. People get sick. . . . Heat stroke and exhaustion are common. There are no guarantees of any sort, including safety or comfort. I must rely on my own luck and positive attitude.

"I understand this is a serious expedition into difficult country. I will be asked to skin down the cargo to a bare minimum. I won't bring extra luxuries, because I understand that when I get hurt, someone else invariably ends up carrying my extra stuff. Also I may need to carry supplies in emergencies, which do occur. I'll accept the suggestions to drink water, and accept suggestions to go slow. We need to travel as a team. This is a group effort.

"I understand everyone is expected to pitch in. The Tarahumaras who accompany us extend our endurance by carrying our stuff, and are paid to do so. But we all pitch in to gather wood, prepare meals, clean up, and fetch water. They are our traveling companions who enjoy the adventure same as us, not our servants . . . . I also understand that we are visitors in the Sierra, which properly belongs to its Tarahumara residents. They have asked us not to photograph them or their homes. I will scrupulously respect their wishes."

laced with footpaths and populated by a well-adapted local culture—it lacks a trekking tradition and infrastructure. Finding a guide and pack animals on your own is a time-consuming process that demands a good command of Spanish. Even on outfitted treks, don't expect clockwork efficiency or morning tea handed through your tent flap. The Tarahumara are not Sherpas; their primary duties are to attend to the pack burros. And if, as happened on one recent Copper Canyon trek, rain dissolves the cardboard boxes containing the live chickens for dinner that night, you will be called upon to carry one of the squawking, squirming entrées-to-be.

Nepal veterans will notice more steep climbs up and over ridges and mesas, and less time spent following river valleys. Vertical gains (and losses) of 5,000 feet a day are possible. The steep ups and downs can be very hard on boots and feet, even for experienced trekkers.

Altitude sickness is not a problem, although you will definitely feel the lack of oxygen as you huff and puff up steep trails in the upper reaches of the canyon. Dehydration, however, can be a very serious problem. Although it looks green, and even lush in some places, Copper Canyon is a desert in

Tarahumara Indians still live in the cliff dwellings they have occupied for centuries.

disguise, with very dry air that sucks moisture right out of you. In the lower reaches, when the temperature can hit 90°F, you'll sweat profusely.

GUIDES AND OUTFITTERS

Copper Canyon is not a place you should trek without a guide. The network of trails is labyrinthine, and there are no trail maps. Moreover, the solo trekker may wander unexpectedly close to Tarahumara dwellings and caves, which can be upsetting to these shy, reclusive people. You may also stumble upon a clandestine marijuana field guarded by its trigger-happy owner.

LOCAL OUTFITTERS

There are local "outfitters" in Creel, the canyon rim gateway town, and Batopilas, in the canyon itself. (We use the term outfitter loosely; they are essentially guys with donkeys who know the way.) Hiking guides range in cost from roughly $10 a day for a green kid to $15–$25 for an experienced guide who may speak a little English. Pack burros cost $5–$10 per day.

To find a local outfitter, check the backpacker hostels and tourist-oriented hotels in Creel or Batopilas. In Creel, Umarike Expeditions and Pedro Palma come recommended by Copper

BATOPILAS

Batopilas, which lies at the bottom of the second-deepest canyon of the Copper Canyon system, is today a quiet river town of 1,100 ranchers, miners, artisans, and assorted shopkeepers, reachable by a twisting, vertiginous dirt road that descends 6,000 feet from the canyon rim. But in its heyday, around the turn of the century, Batopilas was an elegant European-style community of more than 10,000, strung out along a two-mile stretch of the river in the steamy canyon bottom. Its inhabitants built lavish homes and gave elaborate parties, living a life of Victorian luxury and elegance provided them by the wealth from one of the world's richest silver mining dis-

tricts. From the mines at Batopilas, vast treasures were sent out to New York, Paris, and London; pure native silver in pieces that sometimes exceeded 400 pounds.

Overseeing this turn-of-the-century operation was Alexander Shepherd (the last governor of Washington D.C.), who lived in the splendor of a three-story adobe gothic mansion complete with swimming pool, a piano carried eight days from Chihuahua by relays of Tarahumaras, and some of the first electric lights in Mexico. The eerie ruins of his home still stand at the edge of town and are a popular tourist attraction.

—*Keith Albritton*

Canyon veteran Skip McWilliams, proprietor of Copper Canyon Hiking Lodges.

U.S. Outfitters

Several American outfitters run burro-supported treks in Copper Canyon. Remarkable Journeys runs four trips a year along a little-used and quite scenic route from Batopilas to Urique. Adventure Specialists' trips have an archaeological bent. The Copper Canyon Hiking Lodges' expeditions, led by McWilliams, venture well off the usual trails, and are the most rugged and unpredictable of the lot, and would rate a 3 in both physical and mental challenge.

ADVENTURE SPECIALISTS
719-783-2076
$1,370 for 10 days
(This trip can also be booked through GORP, www.gorp.com)

ALL ABOUT ADVENTURE
907-451-8148
www2.ptialaska.net/wildakmx
$1,375 for 9 days

COPPER CANYON HIKING LODGES
800-776-3942
www.coppercanyonlodges.com
$1,400 for 8 days

REMARKABLE JOURNEYS
800-856-1993
www.remjourneys.com
$1,099 for 10 days

RECOMMENDED READING
■ *THE TARAHUMAR OF MEXICO*, Campbell Pennington ($85.30. Books on Demand.) A somewhat dry scholarly study, but still considered the most thorough work on Tarahumara culture. Good description of the kick-ball races.
■ *TARAHUMARA: WHERE NIGHT IS THE DAY OF THE MOON*, Bernard Fontana (1997. $19.95 University of Arizona Press.) A more reader-friendly look at Tarahumara culture and history.

Midday in Batopilas, a village that lies at the bottom of the canyon, 6,000 feet below the rim.

■ *UNKNOWN MEXICO*, Carl Lumholtz ($125.00 AMS Pr.) Classic narrative of a Norwegian explorer's travels in the Sierra Madre during the 1890s.
■ *MEXICO'S COPPER CANYON COUNTRY: A HIKING AND BACKPACKING GUIDE*, John Fayhee (1994. $16.95. Johnson Books.) A breezy, very personal memoir/guidebook for canyon walkers, with a detailed description of the Batopilas-Urique walk.

Inner Dolpo

If it's good enough for Peter Matthiessen and George Schaller, it's good enough for you.

ere's how the story was told to me, by someone who should know. After Mao's invasion of Tibet in 1950, rebellious Khampa tribesmen began a guerrilla war of resistance against the Chinese. Their bases were across the border in the Nepalese districts of Mustang and Dolpo, high, arid, and remote mountain redoubts virtually unchanged since medieval times. The Khampa, a rough-and-ready lot with banditry in their blood, took to kidnapping the Chinese headmen in Tibetan border villages, skinning them, and hanging their remains from poles in the village square. The American CIA liked the sound of that, and supplied the Khampas with automatic rifles and grenade launchers, and trained them in mountain warfare at a base in Colorado.

When the Chinese captured some guerrillas, discovered the American weapons, and learned that the rebels had come from across the border, a

Approaching the "runway" at Juphal, site of Dolpo's only airstrip and the usual entry point for trekkers.

colonel at the Chinese embassy in Kathmandu paid a visit to Nepal's King Mahendra. As the story goes, the colonel made His Royal Highness an offer he couldn't refuse: Either shut down the rebellious Khampa, seal off the border, and close Mustang and Dolpo to all foreigners, or we'll march in and take them away from you. The King assented, and for decades Mustang and Dolpo were off-limits to all but a handful of scholars and naturalists with special dispensations.

But with the end of the Cold War, tensions eased, and Mustang and Dolpo were opened to trekkers in 1992. Mustang and the southern part of Dolpo have since become well-established (if somewhat off-the-beaten-path) trekking areas. But the inner sanctum of the formerly forbidden land—the northern part of Dolpo, known as Inner Dolpo—has remained virtually untracked. In 1999, less than 100 trekkers ventured into Inner Dolpo, only about 40 of them Americans.

The decades-long closure of Inner Dolpo added to its mystery and allure among the few travelers who knew of it. One of the highest and most remote inhabited regions of the world (if three or four thousand people in an area the size of Connecticut can be called inhabited) Inner Dolpo was cut off entirely from the outside world in winter, when snow smothers the few passes into the region. The high, arid jumble of small, steep valleys lies in the "rain shadow" of the Himalayas, protected from the summer monsoons that wash the southern flanks of the range. Even among the Nepalese, Inner Dolpo is considered a mysterious, remote, primitive region. Its rugged terrain and isolation have staved off outside influence for centuries, and allowed it to remain one of the last enclaves of pure Tibetan Buddhist culture.

Inner Dolpo's spiritual centerpiece is a place called Shey, the Crystal Mountain, a small but wildly stratified peak embedded with crystal deposits that glimmer in the sunlight. It was here that a revered 10th-century Tibetan Buddhist teacher, Drutob Senge Yeshe, supposedly arrived on the back of a flying snow lion and defeated a powerful animist mountain god who dwelled there. Meditating in a cave below the mountain, Yeshe subsequently attained perfect enlightenment. A thousand years later, a Tibetan Buddhist

---

AT A GLANCE

TRIP LENGTH 28–38 days	PRICE RANGE (INDEPENDENT TREK) Not permitted
TIME ON TREK 14–31 days	PRICE RANGE (OUTFITTED GROUP TREK)
WALKING DISTANCE 100–200 miles	$5,000–$7,000
MAXIMUM ALTITUDE 18,000 feet	PRIME TIME May–September
PHYSICAL CHALLENGE 1 2 3 4 ⑤	STAGING CITY Kathmandu, Nepal
MENTAL CHALLENGE 1 2 3 4 ⑤	

Prayer flags at Shey Gompa, the spiritual center of Inner Dolpo and site, in the 10th century, of a Tibetan Buddhist teacher's perfect enlightenment.

monastery, called Shey Gompa, and a hermitage at the foot of the mountain are still the heart of Dolpo. Hundreds of pilgrims from all over the region make the annual *kora*, a ritual ten-mile walk around the sacred mountain. The walk finishes in front of Yeshe's meditation cave, at a temple that contains his ashes.

The Dolpo region gained a measure of fame when Peter Matthiessen wrote about it in the best-selling book *The Snow Leopard*. Matthiessen accompanied the naturalist George Schaller on a two-month trek to Shey Gompa in 1973 to study the rare Himalayan blue sheep, or bharal, which was found in great numbers near the monastery

(the lama forbade hunting). The pair also hoped to see the elusive snow leopard, which preys on the sheep. In the end, Matthiessen failed to see a snow leopard, and did not manage to enter the fabled monastery, which had been locked up for the winter. But he saw deep inside himself during his 17 days there, and his spiritual journey of self-discovery became a classic of its kind.

The attractions of this ancient Buddhist enclave are not just spiritual. Trekking along the Suli Gad river, Matthiessen writes of its dark walls and swirling mists, "I wonder if anywhere on earth there is a river more beautiful. . . ." The Suli Gad flows out of an emerald-blue lake called Phoksumdo, a holy sea that has seen neither boat nor bather for the last thousand years. The trail along its shoreline is a breathtakingly narrow cliffside ledge high above the waterline. Matthiessen described his passage along the vertiginous lake trail this way: "Parts of the ledge have fallen away, and the gaps are bridged by flimsy scaffoldings of saplings. Certain sections are so narrow and precarious that more than once my legs refused to move, and my heart beats so that I feel sick. One horrid stretch, lacking the smallest handhold in the wall, rounds a windy point of cliff that is more than one hundred feet above the rocks at lake edge, and this I navigate on hands and knees, arriving a lifetime later. . .at one of the few points in that whole first mile where one can lean far enough into the cliff to let another man squeeze by."

Even Matthiessen's surefooted crew of nine boisterous, talkative Sherpa porters gave the Phoksumdo trail their undivided attention. "At that dangerous point of cliff. . .the nine fall silent in the sudden way that birds are stilled by the shadow of a hawk. . . .On they come, staring straight ahead, as steadily and certainly as ants, yet seeming to glide with an easy ethereal lightness, as if some inner concentration were lifting them just off the surface of the ground. . . .Mute, unknowing, dull eyes glazed, the figures brush past one by one in their wool boots and sashed tunics. . . .

Donkeys at Dunai. Some trekkers walk from Juphal to Dunai, and then continue north to Shey Gompa.

When the bad stretch is past, the hooting instantly resumes. . .as if all had awakened from a trance."

The non-Buddhist trekker on the Phoksumdo Lake trail, unable to summon up the blessed no-mindness to carry him serenely past this fearsome precipice, might well in his moment of agorophobic terror remember the words of Tupjuk Lama, the crippled old monk who had been meditating in the shadow of the Crystal Mountain for eight years when Matthiessen was granted an audience. Asked if he was happy, the lama laughed and looked down at his withered legs. "Of course I am happy here. It's wonderful! Especially when I have no choice!"

BARLEY

Without this hardy grain, human life would not exist in Inner Dolpo. Barley is the only grain that thrives above 10,000 feet, growing at 14,000 feet in some parts of Dolpo. Thousands of varieties grow in Tibet, classified according to their color (red, white, or black), growing time (90 to 130 days), as well as their form and structure (fat or slim, "bearded," or "naked"). Barley is eaten as whole roasted grains, ground into flour, and fermented to make *chang*, the local beer.

Campsite just below Shey Gompa. "Inner Dolpo is the toughest trek in Nepal," according to Fritz Selby, a Nepal hand.

THE ROUTE

Most modern trekkers follow at least some part of the route of Matthiessen and Schaller, who entered Dolpo at Rohagaon, (near Juphal, site of Dolpo's only airstrip and the usual entry point today) and walked north along the Suligad River to Ringmo and Phoksumdo Lake, then continued north over the 17,300-foot Kang La to Shey Gompa. Matthiessen returned via a loop eastward to Saldang and then south along the Nam-Khong Valley and back to Phoksumdo.

Some modern-day treks billed as "Dolpo" treks don't go north of Phoksumdo into Inner Dolpo, where permit fees are much more expensive. (If your objective is to see Shey Gompa and the true Inner Dolpo, check your outfitter's itinerary to make sure.) Outer Dolpo treks, which are much less expensive and more typical of the rest of Nepal, with forests and numerous villages, typically visit Ringmo, the Tarap Valley, and Tarakot.

WHAT TO EXPECT

"Inner Dolpo is the toughest trek in Nepal," says Fritz Selby, an old Nepal hand who walked into the Annapurna sanctuary back in 1960, before commercial trekking in Nepal even existed. "It's very steeply up and down, much more so than the Everest base camp route. The walking can be very hard due to the rocks and scree. And be-cause you're going up and down all the time, altitude acclimatization can be difficult. You've definitely got to be in good shape to trek in Inner Dolpo."

Unlike most other trekking regions of Nepal, you'll not have the feeling of walking among massive, looming ice peaks. Although the passes are as high as 18,000 feet, the highest mountain in Dolpo is "only" about 22,000 feet high. The landscape is arid and bare; you may at times feel you're looking at the world through sepia-colored glasses. Villages are few and far between and the people poor and dirty. To a greater extent than any other area in Nepal, you'll feel as if you've entered a completely new world with no connection to the outside. Even your Sherpas and Nepali camp staff will be astonished at the remoteness and isolation of Dolpo and its people.

GUIDES AND OUTFITTERS

Independent trekking is not permitted in Dolpo, which is still considered a restricted area. Trekkers must travel in groups with an approved trekking company, and each group must be accompanied by a Nepali liaison officer. The route must be preapproved, and no deviations are permitted. And, as a final deterrent to all but the most hard-core trekkers, the permit fee—above and beyond the actual expenses of the trip—is $70 per day.

LOCAL OUTFITTERS

There are several Kathmandu outfitters experienced in the Inner Dolpo region.

GREEN LOTUS TREKKING

www.greenlotustrekking.com

MOUNTAIN TRAVEL NEPAL

www.tigertops.com

U.S. OUTFITTERS

Three U.S. outfitters run trips into Inner Dolpo. Above the Clouds offers what may be the longest (and toughest) commercial trek in the world, a

Top: People of Inner Dolpo displayed prized photos of the Dalai Lama. Above: Dzo carrying supplies on the trail to Phoksumdo Lake.

38-day trip that includes both Inner Dolpo and the neighboring kingdom of Mustang. Snow Lion Expeditions runs a Mustang/Dolpo combo trip similar to Above the Clouds' as well as a trip to Inner Dolpo timed to coincide with the annual pilgrimage. Camp 5's Dolpo/Mustang trek is led by noted guide Alan Burgess.

B'ON

The ancient Tibetan animist cult defeated by the Buddhist mystic Drutob Senge Yeshe at Crystal Mountain (see pages 181-182) lives on today in Dolpo, as a regressive sect of Buddhism called B'on. Several villages, including Ringmo, near Phoksumdo Lake, are predominately B'on, and there is a B'on monastery, Tso Gompa, perched high above the lake.

In its ancient rather bloodthirsty form, B'on required the sacrifice of an animal at a funeral, to accompany the dearly beloved to heaven. When a king died, one of his aides was sacrificed to keep him company.

Ancient B'on legend says that Phoksumdo Lake was formed when a B'on sorceress unleashed a vast flood to destroy a village that had betrayed her.

In its 20th century version, B'on mischievously turns Buddhism on its head. Its symbol is a backwards swastika, the mirror image of the Buddhist symbol. And while Buddhist custom requires that one walk counter-clockwise around any sacred building or monument, B'on requires just the opposite—keep your right shoulder toward the sacred structure when passing it.

ABOVE THE CLOUDS
800-233-4499
www.gorp.com/abvclds
$5,800–$6,750 for 38 days

SNOW LION EXPEDITIONS
800-525-8735
www.snowlion.com
$6,400 for 36 days; $5,100 for 26 days

CAMP 5 EXPEDITIONS
800-914-3834
www.camp5.com
$3,950 for 29 days

A number of outfitters, both in Nepal and the United States offer treks in southern Dolpo that go as far north as Phoksumdo Lake. However, they do not go into Inner Dolpo itself. These treks are only about half the price of the Inner Dolpo treks because the permit fees are much lower.

RECOMMENDED READING (AND VIEWING)

■ *THE SNOW LEOPARD*, Peter Matthiessen (1987. $12.95. Viking Penguin.) An account of the author's two-month trek to Shey Gompa in 1973.

■ *HIMALAYAN PILGRIMAGE*, David Snellgrove Perhaps the world's premiere Tibetologist, Snellgrove traveled extensively in Dolpo in the 1950s. This account of one of his journeys is rich in the history and culture of the region.

■ *CARAVAN* A documentary film by French director Eric Valli that follows the annual migration of a tribe of Dolpo yak-herders.

Saka Gompa, a seldom-visited hillside monastery above Shey Gompa.

El Camino de Santiago

Repent, sinners. All you have to do is walk 460 miles with a seashell around your neck.

A religious pilgrimage may seem an odd choice for one of the world's twenty great treks. In my experience, the modern trekker is typically not the deeply religious sort of person who engages in traditional holy rituals. For many of us, God may be in the details, or the sunsets, or the high windblown summits, but certainly not in dusty hurches filled with statues and relics of men long dead. The path to religious apathy of Jack Hitt, a regular *Outside* contributor and occasional

trekker, is probably fairly typical: ". . .I effortlessly cast off the religion of my parents as if stepping out of a pair of worn trousers," he writes in his book *Off the Road*. "It happened sometime around college back in the 1970s and therefore was done with the casual arrogance and glibness famous to that time. . .my general attitude about religion has mellowed since that time into a courteous indifference. . .if I'm angry or have been drinking, I'm quick to say that when it comes to good will on

The modern pilgrim still carries a staff and a cross, and wears the traditional scallop shell around his neck.

earth, religion has been as helpful as a dead dog in a ditch, and that in this century it's been little more than a repository of empty ritual and a cheap cover for dim-witted bigotries. So imagine the reaction of many of my friends and relatives when I announced that I was going on a pilgrimage. . . ."

And not just any pilgrimage. Hitt had decided to embark on the Camino de Santiago, or the Road of St. James, a 500-mile 1,200-year-old pilgrim's route along the northern tier of Spain from the Pyrenees to the city of Santiago de Compostela, where the (alleged) bones of St. James the Apostle have rested since A.D. 841, when a wandering hermit came across the body in a cave. Over the last 1,200-odd years, untold millions of devout Christians have walked from all over Europe to rub a statue of the saint and to receive deliverance from their sins.

Thousands of people still make the trip each year, all or in part, for a variety of reasons not always related to true faith. Fortunately, St. James was no paragon of virtue himself (Hitt calls him an "incorrigible lickspittle") and his pilgrims have always been a variegated lot. A 12th-century document from a pilgrims' shelter along the route announced that "Its doors are open to all, well and ill, not only to Catholics, but to pagans, Jews, and heretics, the idler and the vagabond. . .the good and the wicked." Like Hitt, most of us can find ourselves in that list somewhere.

A pilgrimage, by definition, lacks a certain adventurous edge. As Hitt put it, "We pilgrims want to believe that we are not tourists. But by whatever definition you want to use, pilgrims are tourists. Pilgrims are the lowest of lowbrow travelers, a subspecies of tourist, the most degraded hybrid there is. Our itinerary is a thousand years old. Our route has been walked millions of times. Far from being the first, a pilgrim is in fact the opposite. With each step, we are precisely the last person to cover that patch of ground. And a few minutes later even that lame distinction will vanish, our footprint trampled by a crowd of schoolchildren, or a mule, or robust senior citizens from Holland." (This was not always so. One 12th-century chronicler of the Camino de Santiago wrote, "How many thousands of pilgrims have died, some lost in snowstorms, others, more numerous still, devoured by the ferocity of wolves.")

AT A GLANCE

Trip Length 10–30 days	Price Range (independent trek)
Time on Trek 8–28 days	$300–$2,000
Walking Distance 120–460 miles	Price Range (outfitted group trek)
Maximum Altitude 4,900 feet	$2,200–$4,200
Physical Challenge ① 2 3 4 5	Prime Time May–June, September–October
Mental Challenge ① 2 3 4 5	(July and August are hot and very crowded)
	Staging City Barcelona, Spain or Toulouse, France

Early in their pilgrimage, trekkers cross this 11th-century bridge at Puente la Reina, ordered constructed for pilgrims by the wife of a Navarrese king.

What exactly, then, is the reward of a pilgrimage for the nonreligious? "The word still had enough of its medieval flavor to suggest that one was submitting to a regime, a task, an idea whose ultimate end would be discovery, even transformation." And yet, lacking even that profound sense of discovery and transformation, a pilgrimage is not without a more familiar sort of adventurous, trekkish appeal: "A pilgrimage was about sweating and walking and participating in something," writes Hitt "One could dress it up with all kinds of rationales and ritual, but stripped down, a pilgrim was a guy out for some cosmically serious fresh air."

The Santiago pilgrim requires a number of special accoutrements. First is the *carnet*, or *Credencial de Peregrino* (Pilgrim's Credential), a small official-looking folded card that serves as the pilgrim's passport. Issued by churches or monasteries along the route, it is stamped nightly at pilgrims' rest houses to document the walker's passage. Upon arrival at Santiago de Compostela,

the passport is presented to the local priest, who then issues a *compostellana*, a grand-looking parchment written in Latin that certifies the completion of the pilgrim's journey. Another vital accessory is the traditional scallop shell—the familiar kind of open fluted shell that serves as the oil company's symbol—typically worn around the neck on a string. The origins of this custom are obscure, but the shell will immediately identify you to locals and to other pilgrims.

Traditional St. James pilgrim garb includes a full-length black cape, a broad-brimmed black hat, a walking staff, and a leather bag worn around the waist. In the early days, pilgrim fashion was strictly regulated, and those so garbed were immune to local laws and entitled to free food and lodging. These days, though, anything goes on the fashion scene, and pilgrims must pay their way like everyone else—although most towns and villages along the route have special pilgrims' hostels, many attached to the local church or monastery, that charge less than $5 per night.

These pilgrim *rifugios* can be quite entertaining. In the village of Torres del Rio, Hitt stayed in a dilapidated mansion presided over by the wild-haired cross-eyed El Ramon, who

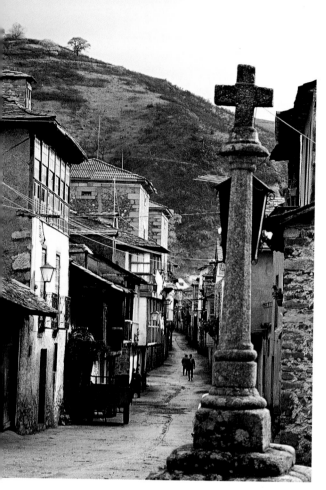

Along the route in the village of Molinaseca on the banks of the Rio Meruelo.

July 25th—the scene at the pilgrim refuges devolves into unseemly scrambling and scheming to claim bunk space. "The pilgrimage takes on a decidedly different complexion now," notes Hitt "The operative metaphor of the lonely drudging hermit has given way to the strategems of Clauswitz. It may be petty, it may be juvenile, but at stake are the basic necessities. So, it's war."

The St. James pilgrim may find salvation and enlightenment, or he may not. But at the very least he'll get some fresh air and exercise, see some beautiful countryside, meet some people very much different from himself, and feel the accomplishment of arriving at a long-sought destination under his own power. At the very least, the pilgrim will simply be. . .a trekker.

THE ROUTE

The traditional Camino de Santiago route has a number of parallel threads that begin in France. The most popular "full" route, which covers 460 miles, begins in the French border town of St. Jean and proceeds through the Pyrenees to the Spanish village of Roncesvalles, and then on to Pamplona. (If you're a glutton for crowds and drunken revelry, time your arrival here with the running of the bulls from July 7 to 14.) The route then proceeds westward through Logrono, Burgos, Leon, and finally on to Santiago de Compostela itself. The route, ostensibly marked with signs and yellow arrows, is a patchwork of footpaths, farm roads, dirt roads, paved highways and even major superhighways for short stretches.

The preceding route can be completed in about 30 days of brisk walking, an average of 15 to 20 miles per day. (The daily mileage is high by trekking standards, but reasonably doable due to the low altitude, moderate terrain, and the availability of food and shelter along the way.) For more leisurely pilgrims strolling along at ten miles a day or less, the trek can take up to two months.

carried on conversations with an imaginary girlfriend, speaking both roles simultaneously. At night, strange whoops and cries emanated from his room (". . .gently, benevolently, but in the end, completely insane," Hitt concluded). In the nearly abandoned village of San Juan de Ortega, a talkative priest named Jose Marie put on a vaudeville routine detailing the history of his monastery and served a divine and mysterious garlic soup. In Villafranca, the innkeeper is named Jesus and the inn consists of a giant two-room tent built of scrap lumber, sheet plastic, and bent nails. During the peak pilgrimage season—leading up to the Festival of St. James in Santiago de Compostela on

Leon, near the halfway point, was founded as a Roman garrison. The path here is marked with original bronze scallop shells.

The vast majority of modern-day Santiago pilgrims don't complete the full route. Popular starting points for shorter mini-pilgrimages include Burgos and Leon. From these two points on, the route will become noticeably more crowded with quickie one-and two-week pilgrims. Most group outfitted treks marketed as Camino de Santiago pilgrimages start in Burgos or Leon and skip major portions of the route, concentrating on the most scenic and historic sections. These are really walks rather than treks. They are certainly not pilgrimages.

WHAT TO EXPECT

This is not a wilderness or solitary experience. Along with the rolling meadows, quiet forests, and quaint villages with millennium-old churches, you'll also pass through boring flat farmland, blah suburbs, and gritty industrial areas. Much of the time you'll see other people, either fellow pilgrims along the trail, or local villagers and townspeople. If being part of a crowd bothers you, try another trek. (Being part of a historical crowd of several million people, in fact, is the whole idea.)

The centuries-old Camino is well marked.

It's possible to camp out or stay in semi-luxurious hotels and paradors—inns of a certain standard of charm and amenities certified by the Spanish government—along the way. But most people stay in pilgrims' *rifugios*, basic hostels with bunk beds and communal eating and bathroom facilities. Independent trekkers will have to carry small backpacks with sleeping bag, clothes, and personal gear, but no food or camping equipment.

GUIDES AND OUTFITTERS

A support system for independent Camino de Santiago trekkers has been well in place for about 1,200 years now. Every 10 miles or so, there's a pilgrim's refuge that typically costs $3 to $5 per night. (You must show your official pilgrim's passport to get in.) With monklike devotion to minimalist principles you can do this trek for as little as $10 a day, without camping. A more reasonable independent trekking budget might be $25 per day. A guide is unnecessary; if you get lost, simply ask a local, they have a lifelong familiarity with wandering pilgrims.

At the upper end of the outfitter scale, The British company ATG Oxford offers a 15-day walking trip along the full length of the Camino that skips the dull sections. Walkers stay in upscale hotels and inns. Several U.S. outfitters offer shorter full-service walks along some of the more scenic sections of the Camino. Typically, you'll be bussed to and from the Camino route each day, "cherry-picking" the nicest parts of the route and returning to a substantial hotel or parador each night. Although these give a nice taste of the Camino, the truncated route and upscale accommodations miss the point of the pilgrimage, and don't qualify as treks.

THE HIGHEST ROAD

It's probably safe to say that no other trek in this book can offer the rewards promised to the Camino de Santiago pilgrim. The *Codex Calixtinus*, which contains a 12th-Century guidebook to the Camino, lists the many benefits of the month-long trek: "It takes one away from succulent foods, makes voracious obesity disappear, restrains voluptuousness, contains the appetites of the flesh which attack the fortress of the soul, purifies the spirit, invites man to the contemplative life, humbles the haughty, raises up the humble, loves poverty. It hates the censure of the man dominated by avarice. It loves, on the other hand, the person who gives to the poor. It rewards the austere who do good works; and, on the other hand, it does not snatch the miserly and sinful from the talons of sin."

Pamplona's famous running of the bulls, held every July, is an excuse for much unchristian revelry.

ATG OXFORD
800-527-5997
$4,165 for 15 days

CAMINO TOURS
800-938-9311
www.webtravel.com/caminotour
$2,250 for 8 days

PROGRESSIVE TRAVELS
800-245-2229
www.progressivetravels.com
$2,250 for 8 days

RECOMMENDED READING

■ *CODEX CALIXTINUS.* This may be the world's first European travel guidebook—a 12th Century Baedeker that describes the Camino de Santiago in exhaustive detail. (A translation by William Melczer is entitled *The Pilgrim's Guide to Santiago de Compostela.* 1993. $17.50. Italian Press.)

■ *OFF THE ROAD: A MODERN-DAY WALK DOWN THE PILGRIM'S ROUTE INTO SPAIN,* Jack Hitt (1994. $10.95. Simon & Schuster.) A hilarious account of the author's two-month, 500-mile pilgrimage along the Camino de Santiago.

■ *WALKING IN SPAIN,* Miles Roddis et al (1999. $17.95. Lonely Planet.) A Lonely Planet guide with a 34-page section on the Camino. The route described is a 28-day 460-mile walk starting in Roncesvalles.

The Northwest Frontier

*"I've been all over the world, and that's the only place
I ever cried when I had to leave."*

Jackie Steakley was thrilled when an Argentine couple came into her jewelry gallery in Carmel, California, one day a few years ago. A veteran Nepal trekker and world traveler, she had just signed up for an Andes trek in the remote northwestern corner of Argentina, in the frontier province of Jujuy. The outfitter's catalog had rhapsodized about isolated, austerely beautiful mountains and amiable local people little touched by modern ways. Eagerly she pumped the Argentine couple for information. Have you ever been there? How's the scenery? What are the people like?

The Argentine couple looked at her aghast. Jujuy? You're going to Jujuy? Nobody ever goes there they told her. . .There's no reason to go there, nothing to do, nothing to see—just Indians. Go to Bariloche," they advised. "Go to Fitzroy. See the beautiful parts of our country. Don't waste your time on Jujuy. We're ashamed of that place.

Dismissed by Argentinians, Jujuy is a remote province of fantastic colors peopled by descendants of the Inca.

BOLIVIA

CHILE

JUJUY PROVINCE

ARGENTINA

That's not Argentina, that's Bolivia!"

Steakley shakes her head and laughs when she recalls the incident today. "They were right about one thing—nobody ever goes there—but totally wrong about everything else. I've been all over the world, and that's the only place I ever cried when I had to leave."

Partly it was the land itself, high arid country called *puna* in the Quechuan language, dotted with *ichu* grass and punctuated by 16,000-foot mountains and stark canyons. The landscape is slashed by striking bands of alternating colors: oranges and reds mixed with sandy pastels and a rainbow of greens—grey-green, blue-green, green-green. "Never have I seen such colors," reports another trekker, a connoisseur of the American Southwest. "There is no way those colors can be captured on film, or even by a painter. And any attempt to describe them with words would be ludicrous." In that case, let's move on to the real reason Jackie Steakley broke into tears upon leaving: the local people.

Descendants of the Inca, the Collas Indians live in the end-of-the-road town of Iruya and 25 surrounding villages that are reachable only by foot. Almost from the moment of their arrival in Iruja, Steakley and her trekmates were overwhelmed by the friendliness of the Collas. Children scampered around them, laughing with sparkling brown eyes. But unlike the well-practiced beggar children of Nepal, who beseech trekkers with shouts of "Rupee!" Bon-bon!" and "Pen!," the Collas ragamuffins demanded from their visitors only the chance to hold hands and talk.

Steakley remembers two girls, six or seven years old, who walked to an orchard outside of town, picked a small basket of white peaches, then walked back to the local guesthouse, where they sat on the stoop to wait for a trekker to emerge. An hour later, when Steakley appeared, the girls shyly pushed the peaches into her hands and ran off giggling.

On another occasion, when the outfitter's Renault van broke down on the dirt road to Iruya, children with outstretched arms surrounded the group, offering necklaces and other local handicrafts. When the trekkers reflexively pulled wads of pesos from their pockets, the children shook

AT A GLANCE

TRIP LENGTH 12–16 days	PRICE RANGE (INDEPENDENT TREK)
TIME ON TREK 5–7 days	Not available
WALKING DISTANCE 35–45 miles	PRICE RANGE (OUTFITTED GROUP TRK)
MAXIMUM ALTITUDE 13,100 feet	$1,800–$2,500
PHYSICAL CHALLENGE 1 2 ③ 4 5	PRIME TIME March, October, November
MENTAL CHALLENGE 1 2 ③ 4 5	STAGING CITY Buenos Aires, Argentina

Collas Indian girls in adobe doorway. Living in villages reachable only on foot, they are innocently friendly.

their heads. "Don't you understand? We want nothing from you. These are gifts!"

The Collas villages are populated mainly by women and children: The men spend most of the year in distant sugarcane fields and towns, working for cash wages. When the men do come home, they like to celebrate. One group of trekkers happened into the village of San Juan during the Day of the Cross celebration and found every male in town dead drunk. Constitutionally incapable of selfishness even in their alcoholic stupor and horizontal repose, the men, upon seeing the visitors, offered up from the gutters their remaining corn whiskey. There were no takers.

There were many takers, however, for the coca leaves that the trip leader, the perpetually smiling Luis Aguilera, handed out to group members at moments of duress. Whatever the complaint—jet lag, altitude sickness, agorophobia on the precarious trails—Luis' reply was always the

Opposite and overleaf:"The landscape is slashed by bands of colors: oranges and reds mixed with sandy pastels and a rainbow of greens—grey-green, blue-green, green-green...."

same: "Suck on this." He would pull from his pack a fistful of coca leaves, to be either brewed up in tea or inserted 'twixt the cheek and gum like a wad of chewing tobacco. Coca leaves, which are of course the raw material for cocaine, have been used by Andean mountain people for centuries to make the wretched days of poverty go by a little faster. "I felt euphoric," reported one trekker. "It took the edge off," said another. Steakley, phobic about riding in vehicles on narrow, twisting mountain roads, chewed the coca leaves and found an eerie inner calm. "A miracle," she says.

The coca leaves did not, however, cure a hacking cough that Steakley developed in the dry, dusty air. For that, she visited a village market, where a *bruja*—a female witch doctor—mixed up a custom cure. The *bruja*, an elderly woman with piercing eyes and a limited number of teeth, listened carefully as Steakley described her symptoms. Then, as Steakley tells it, "she started grabbing stuff from various bags around her. The mix included several varieties of dried leaves, a chopped-up llama fetus, and a number of weird shriveled-up carcasslike things with eyes and beaks." The *bruja* ordered Steakley to brew tea from the mixture and drink three cups of it. Steakley nodded politely, but in the end could not bring herself to comply.

Most nights, the trekkers camped near villages, often in schoolyards. The local women would drift by the camp, joining the trekkers for dinner and talking late into the night about the hardships of life in these valleys: avalanches, flash floods, child-eating pumas, witches. They revealed methods for increasing their husbands' fertility (get a magic pebble from the *bruja* and slip it into bed) and their opinions of the local Catholic missionaries. ("They're gossips, so in confession, we never tell them the truth. We make up all sorts of wild stuff to keep them occupied.")

In light of the otherwise guileless nature of the Collas, such small deceptions may be forgiven. "They are the kindest, most unspoiled people I've ever seen," sighs Steakley. "I still can't figure out why nobody goes there."

THE ROUTE

The outfitted trips listed here start in Buenos Aires. Trekkers fly to either Salta or Jujuy, then drive north into the mountains to the end-of-the-road town of Iruya. (On the way, you'll drive through Quebrada de Humahuaca, a deep canyon sprinkled with villages, and cross a 13,000-foot pass.) From Iruya, trekkers make a five-day or seven-day loop into the mountains, passing through San Juan and a number of other isolated villages. Southwind

CONDOR CARRION

The hot sun and deep valleys of the *puna* create powerful updrafts, the primary habitat requirement for the world's largest flying bird, the Andean condor. The huge creatures, whose wings span about 10 feet, often buzz trekkers along the trail, blotting out the sun and giving off an audible whoosh as they pass as low as 20 feet overhead. "You kind of jump when the shadow goes over you," reports one trekker. "It's huge. At first you think it's an airplane." Such low-level passes are most likely just curiosity about a new species of biped, but the darker possibility of preprandial reconnaissance cannot be discounted. Villagers have seen condors dive-bomb lambs on clifftops, apparently in hopes of distracting them into a fatal slip and dining on the ensuing carrion. "We kept yelling up at them 'Hey, man, we're alive! You can't eat us!'"

"Burros carry the loads, and you may find yourself quite enamored of the cuddly little creatures."

clients return to Salta for the flight back to Buenos Aires. Above the Clouds clients take a three-day tour before flying back to Buenos Aires, with excursions to the nearby Bolivian border town of La Quiaca and Lago Pozuelos, a lake set below a string of volcanoes.

WHAT TO EXPECT

This is not a difficult trek—modest altitude, with an average daily walking distance of seven miles. Most days demand only 1,000 to 2,000 feet of elevation gain, although there's one 3,000-foot day. However, some of the trails are

Most days of trekking demand only 1,000 to 2,000 feet of elevation gain, although there's one 3,000-foot day.

quite exposed, with drop-offs up to 2,000 feet. A couple of the river crossings will get your full attention.

Burros carry the loads, and you may find yourself quite enamored of the cuddly little creatures. The weather is hot and dry, and with the altitude, there is a real danger of dehydration.

Both outfitters use the same trip leader, Salta resident Luis Aguilera, a Buenos Aires native and mountain climber who passed through the area on the way to a mountain, fell in love with the landscape and people, and moved to Salta. (His wife Maru usually goes along on treks as the cook.) Luis has been roaming these canyons for 15 years and always brings gifts of food, tools, and medicine to the local people. As a result, he is much loved in these mountains. For the locals, any friend of Luis' is

a friend of theirs who will be welcomed as an honored guest. And, since only two or three trekking groups a year pass through the area, the local people have remained comparatively unspoiled by contact with foreigners.

GUIDES AND OUTFITTERS

Independent trekking is very difficult here. There is no trekking infrastructure at all—no guides (other than Luis), no professional burro packers, nada. And of course no one speaks any English. When Luis has a trek scheduled, he must send a runner into one of the remote villages to alert the owners of the burros, a friend of his, to meet him at a prescribed time and place. And of course the independent trekker would miss out on all the good will and local knowledge that Luis provides.

LOCAL OUTFITTERS

No Argentine outfitters run treks into the *puna*, simply because there's zero demand for it in the country—no self-respecting Buenos Aires city-slicker would be caught dead wandering around what they consider to be a poor, backward, desolate, and utterly boring place. Only oddly misguided foreigners seem to have any interest in it.

U.S. OUTFITTERS

Above the Clouds created the trek and enlisted Luis Aguilera to lead it in 1994. Southwind jumped on the bandwagon (a very small bandwagon, to be sure) in 1999.

ABOVE THE CLOUDS
800-233-4499
www.gorp.com/abvclds.htm
$2,250–$2,500 for 16 days

SOUTHWIND ADVENTURES
800-377-9463
www.southwindadventures.com
$1,795–$2,245 for 12 days

RECOMMENDED READING

Sorry, no recommended reading. This area is so remote and unknown that nothing has ever been written about it.

High arid country called puna in the Quechuan language, it is dotted with cactus.

OUTFITTERS

ABOVE THE CLOUDS
800-233-4499
P.O. Box 388
Hinesburg, VT 05461
gorp.com/abvclds.htm
info@aboveclouds.com

ADVENTURE CENTER
800-227-8747
1311 63rd Street
Suite 200
Emeryville, CA 94608
adventure-center.com
ex@adventure-center.com

ADVENTURE GUIDES INTERNATIONAL
Curt Hewitt
612-382-8991
10181--90th Avenue
Milaca, MN 56353
adventureguidesintl.com
info@AdventureGuidesIntl.com

ADVENTURES INTERNATIONAL INC.
800-247-1263
P.O. Box 1006
Hood River, OR 97031
adventuresintl.com
info@adventuresintl.com

ADVENTURE SPECIALISTS
719-783-2519
Bear Basin Ranch
Westcliffe, CO 81252
adventurspec.com
discovery@AdventurSpec.com

AFRICA ADVENTURE COMPANY
800-882-9453
5353 North Federal Highway
Suite 300
Fort Lauderdale, FL 33308
africa-adventure.com
noltingaac@aol.com

ALL ABOUT ADVENTURE
800-598-1076, 907-451-8148
P.O. Box 84651
Fairbanks, AK 99708
ptialaska.net/~wildakmx
wildakmx@ptialaska.net

ALPINE ASCENTS INTERNATIONAL
206-378-1927
121 Mercer Street
Seattle, WA 98109
alpineascents.com
climb@alpineascents.com

AMERICAN WILDERNESS EXPERIENCE
800-444-0099
10055 Westmoor Drive
Suite 215
Westminster, CO 80021
gorptravel.com
dwiggins@gorptravel.com

ANDES ADVENTURES
310-395-5265
1323-12th Street
Suite F
Santa Monica, CA 90491
andesadventures.com
info@andesadventures.com

BACKROADS
800-462-2848
501 Cedar Street
Berkeley, CA 94710
backroads.com
backtalk@backroads.com

BILL RUSSELL'S MOUNTAIN TOURS
800-669-4453
404 Hulls Highway
Southport, CT 06490
russelltours.com
hiking@russelltours.com

BUTTERFIELD & ROBINSON
800-678-1147
70 Bond Street
Toronto, Ontario M5B 1X3
butterfieldandrobinson.com
info@butterfield.com

CAMINO TOURS
800-938-9311
7044 Northeast 18th
Seattle, WA 98115
caminotours.com
info@caminotours.com

CAMP 5 EXPEDITIONS
800-914-3834
9 Exchange Place
Suite 900
Salt Lake City, UT 84111
camp5.com
info@camp5.com

CONCORDIA EXPEDITIONS
719-395-9191
P.O. Box 4159
Buena Vista, CO 81211
concordiaexpeditions.com
info@concordiaexpeditions.com

COPPER CANYON HIKING LODGES
800-776-3942
2741 Paldan Drive
Auburn Hills, MI 48326
coppercanyonlodges.com
coppercanyon@earthlink.net

DISTANT JOURNEYS
888-845-5781
P.O. Box 1211
Camden, ME 04843-1211
distantjourneys.com
ejourney@midcoast.com

ESCALANTE CANYON OUTFITTERS
888-326-4453
P.O. Box 1330
Boulder, UT 84716
ecohike.com
ecohike@color-country.net

EXODUS
011-44-20-8675-5550; 20-8673-0859
9 Weir Road
London SW12 0LT
United Kingdom
exodustravels.co.uk
sales@exodustravels.co.uk

EXPLORE WORLDWIDE
011-44-1252-760000
1 Frederick Street
Aldershot, Hants GU11 1LQ
United Kingdom
explore.co.uk

FOOTPRINT TOURS
011-64-3-548-0145
Box 7027
Nelson, New Zealand
greenkiwi.co.nz/footprints
info@greenkiwi.co.nz

FORUM INTERNATIONAL TRAVEL
800-252-4475
91 Gregory Lane
Suite 21
Pleasant Hill, CA 94523
foruminternational.com
fti@foruminternational.com

GAP ADVENTURES
800-692-5495
19 Duncan Street
Suite 401
Toronto, Ontario M5H 3H1
www.gap.ca
adventure@gap.ca

GEOGRAPHIC EXPEDITIONS
800-777-8183
2626 Lumbard Street
San Francisco, CA 94123
geoex.com
info@geoex.com

HIMALAYAN HIGH TREKS
800-455-8735
241 Dolores Street
San Francisco, CA 94103
himalayanhightreks.com
info@himalayanhightreks.com

HIMALAYAN KINGDOMS LTD.
011-44-117-923-7163
20 The Mall
Clifton, Bristol
BS8 4DR
United Kingdom
himalayankingdoms.com

HIMALAYAN TRAVEL
800-225-2380
110 Prospect Street
Stamford, CT 06901
gorp.com/himtravel.htm
himalayantravel@cshore.com

IBEX EXPEDITIONS
800-842-8139
2657 West 28th Avenue
Eugene, OR 97405-1461
atrav.com/ibex/
ibex@atrav.com

JOURNEYS INTERNATIONAL
800-255-8735
107 Aprill Drive
Suite 3
Ann Arbor, MI 48103-1903
journeysinternational.com
info@journeys-intl.com

KE ADVENTURE TRAVEL
800-497-9675
1131 Grand Avenue
Glenwood Springs, CO 81601
keadventure.com
ketravel@rof.net

LATIN AMERICAN ESCAPES
800-510-5999
712 Bancroft Avenue
PMB #421
Walnut Creek, CA 94598
latinamericanescapes.com
travel@latinamericanescapes.com

LOST WORLD ADVENTURES
800-999-0558
112 Church Street
Decatur, GA 30030
lostworldadventures.com
info@lostworldadventures.com

MILFORD TRACK GUIDED WALK
011-643-441-1138
P.O. Box 259
Queenstown, New Zealand
new-zealand.com/MilfordTrack
mtinfo@milfordtrack.co.nz

MOUNTAIN TRAVEL-SOBEK
888-687-6235
6420 Fairmount Avenue
El Cerrito, CA 94530
mtsobek.com
info@mtsobek.com

NATIVE TRAILS
800-884-3107
6440 Airport Road #C
El Paso, TX 79925
nativetrails.com
nativet@aol.com

PENNY PITOU TRAVEL
800-552-4661
55 Canal Street
Laconia, NH 03246
pennypitoutravel.com
kimt@pennypitoutravel.com

RARE EARTH EXPLORATIONS
212-686-7411
10 Waterside Plaza, 4K
New York, NY 10010-2610
gorp.com/rareearth
ninaroa@wildindia.com

RED ROCK & LLAMAS TOURS
435-559-7325
P.O. Box 1304
Boulder, UT 84716
gorp.com/redrock
rllamas@color-country.net

REI ADVENTURES
800-622-2236
6750 South 228th Street
Kent, WA 98032
rei.com/travel
travel@rei.com

REMARKABLE JOURNEYS
800-856-1993
P.O. Box 31855
Houston, TX 77231-1855
remjourneys.com
cooltrips@remjourneys.com

SAFARICENTRE
800-223-6046
12504 Riverside Drive
N. Hollywood, CA 91607
safaricentre.com
info@safaricentre.com

SHERPA EXPEDITIONS
011-44-20-8577-2717
131a Heston Road
Hounslow, England
TW4 0RF
United Kingdom
realadventure.com

SNOW LION EXPEDITIONS
800-525-8735
350 South 400 East
Suite G2
Salt Lake City, UT 84111
snowlion.com
info@snowlion.com

SOUTHWIND ADVENTURES
800-377-9463
P.O. Box 621057
Littleton, CO 80162
southwindadventures.com
info@southwindadventures.com

SUMMITS ADVENTURE TRAVEL
360-569-2992
Box W
Ashford, WA 98304
summitsadventure.com
info@summitsadventure.com

THOMSON SAFARIS
800-235-0299
347 Broadway
Cambridge, MA 02139
thomsonsafaris.com
info@thomsonsafaris.com

TIGER MOUNTAIN
011- 977-1-411225
P.O. Box 242
Lazimpat
Kathmandu, Nepal
tigertops.com
info@tigermountain.com

TREKSIKKIM
212-996-1758
P.O. Box 7046
Yorkville Station
New York, NY 10128-0010
gorp.com/rareearth/wildindia/sikkim/about.htm
treksikkim@worldnet.att.net

WALKING SOFTLY ADVENTURES
888-743-0723
P.O. Box 86273
Portland, OR 97286
www.wsadventures.com
info@wsadventures.com

WILDERNESS TRAVEL
800-368-2794
1102 9th Street
Berkeley, CA 94710
wildernesstravel.com
info@wildernesstravel.com

WILD FRONTIERS
011-27-11-702-2035
P.O. Box 844
Halfway House
Gauteng, South Africa 1685
wildfrontiers.com
wildfront@icon.co.za

WORLDWIDE ADVENTURES
800-387-1483
1170 Sheppard Avenue West
Suite 45
Toronto, Ontario M3K 2A3
worldwidequest.com
travel@worldwidequest.com

SELECTED SOURCES

CHAPTER ONE Gokyo & Everest Base Camp
H. W. Tilman, *Nepal Himalaya*
Eric Shipton, *That Untraveled World*

CHAPTER THREE Snow Lake
Martin Conway, *Climbing and Exploration in the Karakoram-Himalayas.* 1894. London: T. F. Unwin.

CHAPTER FOUR The Paine Circuit
George Gaylord Simpson, *Attending Marvels: A Patagonian Journal.* 1982. Chicago: University of Chicago Press.

Lady Florence Dixie, *Across Patagonia.* 1880. R. Bentley & Son.

Eric Shipton, *Land of Tempest.* Seattle: The Mountaineers.

CHAPTER SIX The Ruwenzori
H. M. Stanley, *Through the Dark Continent.* 1878. New York: Harper & Bros.

CHAPTER SEVEN Ladakh: Across Zanskar
Helena Norberg-Hodge, *Ancient Futures: Learning from Ladakh.* 1992. Sierra Club.

CHAPTER NINE The Inca Trail
Pedro de Cieza de Leon, translated by Harriet de Onis, *The Incas.* 1959. University of Oklahoma Press.

CHAPTER ELEVEN The Haute Route
Edward Whymper, *Scrambles Among the Alps.* 1996. New York: Dover.

CHAPTER TWELVE The High Atlas
C.E. Andrews, *Old Morocco and the Forbidden Atlas.* 1922. London: George H. Doran Co

CHAPTER FIFTEEN The Darien Gap
? Au (Wade Davis) mentioned in text but no book title

CHAPTER NINETEEN El Camino de Santiago
Jack Hitt, *Off the Road: A Modern-Day Walk Down the Pilgrim's Route into Spain.* 1994. New York: Simon and Schuster.

PHOTO CREDITS

José Azel/Aurora & Quanta Productions: 25, 192

Franco Barbagallo: 32-33, 146 (both), 148, 149, 150, 151, 152

Andrea Booher/Tony Stone Images: 108

Dugald Bremner: 29

Skip Brown: 63, 67, 174 (both), 178, 179

Robert Caputo/Aurora & Quanta Productions: 78 (top), 82 (bottom), 83, 85

Neil Cooper/Panos Pictures: 136

DDB Photography: 105, 196 (both), 198, 199, 200-201, 203, 204, 205

Ulrich Doering/Panos Pictures: 48 (bottom)

Jean-Léo Dugast/Panos Pictures: 128 (top), 131, 135

Blaine Harrington: 8, 19, 94 (both), 96, 98, 99 (both), 100, 102 (center), 107, 112 (top), 114, 115, 116 (both), 117, 120 (center), 123, 127 (top), 130, 132, 133

Bill Hatcher: 154 (both), 157, 158 (both), 159, 160, 161, 172 (center)

Johanna Huber/SIME: 68 (center), 71, 74-75, 77

Gabriel Jecan/Tony Stone Images: 65

Robin Karpan/DDB Photography: 172 (top), 175, 177

Robb Kendrick/Aurora & Quanta Productions: 15

Ace Kvale: 12, 22, 112 (center), 164-165

David McLain/Aurora & Quanta Productions: 88-89, 90, 91, 92, 93

David Noland: 21, 162 (both), 167 (both), 168, 169 (bottom), 170

Barbara Rowell: 104

Galen Rowell: 6, 26, 36, 37 (bottom), 38, 41, 43, 46, 50, 64, 102 (top), 118, 138 (both), 140, 141, 143, 144

Colin Samuels: 97, 101, 110

Kevin Schafer: 66

Marc Schlossman/Panos Pictures: 47, 48 (top), 51

Frederick Selby: 180 (both), 182, 183, 184, 185 (both), 186

Giovanni Simeone: 18, 70, 122, 188 (both), 190-191, 193, 194, 195

Cameron Wake: 54, 55, 56, 57 (both), 58 (both), 59

Beth Wald: 60 (center), 62, 72, 111

Beth Wald/Aurora & Quanta Productions: 106

Gordon Wiltsie: 9, 14, 30, 34 (center), 37 (top), 40, 42, 52 (center), 86 (center), 127 bottom

Art Wolfe/Tony Stone Images: 126 (center)

Ray Wood/Panos Pictures: 78 (center), 80, 81, 82 (top)

Jake Wyman: 11, 44 (center), 49

INDEX